Puppy Steps

Practical Training for Your New Best Friend

D1452973

Puppy Steps

Practical Training for Your New Best Friend

By Libby Rockaway

Libby's Loving Leashes

Puppy Steps
www.PuppyStepsBook.com

FIRST EDITION

ISBN: 978-1-942557-55-5
Published by Clovercroft Publishing, Franklin, Tennesse in association with LLL Publishing, Nicholasville, Kentucky

Cover Photos: Jeannie Francis Photography
Cover Design: Monk Design
Interior Design: Joan Greenblatt
Interior Art: Ibis Lagumbay Art Studio

Photo Credits:
4-H Dog Club, Rally, Swimming, and Fetch - Nancy Snyder
Puppy Biting - Erik Young
Working Group - Nata Sdobnikova/Shutterstock
Terrier Group - Dmitry Kalinovsky/Shutterstock
Sporting Group - Iakov Filimonov/Shutterstock
Nonsporting Group - Eric Isselee/Shutterstock
Hound Group - Erik Lam/Shutterstock
Herding Group - Eric Isselee/Shutterstock
Dock Diving - James E. Knopf/Shutterstock
Disc Dog - Andraz Cerar/*Shutterstock*
Tug of War - Grey Feather/*BigStock*
Jack Russell - Life on White/*BigStock*
Author Signing at Farmers Market - Brian Clark

To Kathy Burgess, with thanks for all

the opportunities she and her

Comfort Retrievers® have given me.

TABLE OF CONTENTS

8

This book is intended for new puppy owners, and (ideally) new pups that are less than four months old. My system is unique — it lets you train your newly acquired puppy quickly and positively.

Puppies are capable of learning so much when they are very young! In fact, training puppies while they are young prevents them from forming bad habits and makes your life much easier and more pleasant as your pup grows up.

Over the last four years, I have trained more than 40 puppies using my method. My system keeps them happy and learning. The puppy training videos on my YouTube page, the *Puppy Steps* channel, and the chart on the next page demonstrate how well my training works — you can have a fully trained puppy in just a few weeks!

Aside from the training of obedience commands, there are some things you need to know in order to best understand how to interact with your pup. Be sure to start the book from the beginning for best results; resist the urge to skip ahead to certain chapters.

Happy training!

10

Puppy Prep Achievement Chart

**All puppies learn at different speeds.
This is an average of the puppies I've trained.**

After	Come	Sit	Down	Stand	Stay	Kennel	Heel	House Training
1 week	A	A	A	U	S	C	C	N
10 days	A	A	A	U	U	S	S	C
2 weeks	BP	BP	BP	A	A	S	U	C
3 weeks	BP	BP	BP	A	A	U	A	S
1 month	BP	BP	BP	BP	A	A	A	S
2 months	BP	BP	BP	BP	BP	BP	A	U
3 months	BP	BP	BP	BP	BP	BP	BP	A

N	NONE
C	CONCEPTUAL
S	SOMETIMES
U	USUALLY
A	ALWAYS
BP	"BOMB PROOF" (Performs even with distractions)

11

Chapter 1

- Early bonding
- First week example schedule

The First Few Days

Early bonding

You've brought your puppy home!

The first few days are all about demonstrating that his new home is a safe, fun place with good food. Days include frequent trips outside along with lots of love, play, protection, but no freedom.

For the first 24 hours with your new puppy simply focus on bonding with him. At the beginning, Fido will be scared and confused, as he has just left his family and all he knows. Help him feel as comfortable as possible while he is getting accustomed to his new environment. This first day he may be unusually calm, use it to your advantage — cuddle! Touch his paws, ears, teeth, etc. Rub his belly — this gets him accustomed to you handling him in a soft, comforting way.

Have multiple toys he can play with, and initiate play. Gently roll a ball across the ground to see if he is interested. Or play with a rope teasingly; maybe he will be interested in pouncing on it. Initiating play will greatly help your bond — Fido will see you as fun!

Let your pup accompany you almost everywhere you go. Unless your pup is in his crate, have him on your lap or next to you on a leash — as you do chores, eat meals, watch TV, do homework on the floor or other work at a desk.

Your pup should always be on a leash within someone's sight, in someone's arms, or in his crate. Puppies need a lot of sleep, so when he seems tired, put him in his crate for a nap. As soon as he wakes up, take him outside to relieve himself and play, then bring him back in and keep him on his leash.

Be thinking about your new buddy's needs and your typical day; begin to formulate a schedule that will suit you both.

The more you care for and handle your pup at the beginning, and the more you associate yourself with good things, the stronger the bond between you and your dog will be.

First week example schedule

 **6:30 a.m.**

Immediately go outside
20 minutes of playing
5 minutes of training
Breakfast
Plays by himself on a leash by me
    while I get ready for the day

 **7:45 a.m.**

Potty break
Crate time

 **10:00 a.m.**

Potty break
10 minutes of play
5 minutes of training
Potty break
Crate time

 **12:00 p.m.**

Potty break
20 minute walk
5 minutes of training
Lunch
Potty break
Crate time

 **3 p.m.**

40-minute walk
10 minutes of training
Plays on a leash or in a playpen near me while I work
Periodically play with puppy
Potty break each hour for the rest of the evening

 **7:30 p.m.**

10 minutes of training
Dinner
Potty break each hour
Plays or sleeps on a leash beside
  me while watching TV

 **10:00 p.m.**

Final potty break
Bedtime in crate

 **2:00 a.m.**

May need a potty break for the first few nights until he gets to be 9 or 10 weeks old.

Frequent naps in the crate are important for Fido; he needs the physical rest and you need rest from the constant effort caring for him requires.

Chapter 2

Your dog training foundation

1. Manage the situation
2. Think ahead
3. Giving treats = Giving feedback
4. Remove and replace
5. Puppy steps forward
6. Puppy steps back!
7. Short and frequent training
8. Only give a command once
9. One command at one time
10. He's smart, but not that smart
11. Being cute is not a trick!
12. Praise.
13. Consistency and expectations
14. How to give commands
15. Commands to use
16. Command sequence
17. Patience
18. Trainer attitude
19. Negative and positive attention
20. Socialization

20 Fundamentals

Dogs like to be trained. What's not to like? Their person is interacting with them and giving them cookies. How fun is that? Good training is like a date with your dog — soon the two of you will fall in love! Some basic factors will keep the two of you connected:

1. Manage the situation

Management is the most important factor when raising a puppy. You must think ahead about timing and consequences. If your puppy makes a mistake, 99 percent of the time you are to blame — you forgot to take him outside, you didn't exercise him enough or perhaps you never taught him a more appropriate behavior.

Keep this in mind in everything you do with your puppy — especially when housebreaking. You must take your pup outside often, keep him close at all times and watch his body language to help get him in the habit of relieving himself outside. Then he will learn to follow the pattern you set.

The key is in the management of his environment so that he rarely has an opportunity to do the wrong thing. Properly handled puppies are always in their crates, on a leash, in your arms, or training. Until they learn to come when called and are fully housebroken, letting them run free is just a problem waiting to happen.

2. Think ahead

Don't allow a behavior to continue unless you want it to continue for the next 12 years of Fido's life. Think about what you want your life with your dog to be like in the future, rather than focusing on how cute the puppy is while he is misbehaving. As soon as Fido presents a behavior for the first time, either encourage it (if it's good) or discourage it (if it isn't).

▲ *For example:* It might be really cute that your 8-week-old, 10-pound puppy is jumping up on your legs because he's happy to see you, but think of Fido as a grown 100-pound dog jumping up on you with muddy paws right when you are about to go out to dinner. Be forward-thinking from the very beginning.

20

2

3. Giving treat = Giving feedback

Giving treats is giving feedback. If Fido gets a treat, you are telling him, "Good! That's what I wanted. Keep doing that." If he doesn't get a treat, you are saying, "Oops, not quite. Try something different." A treat is giving Fido feedback to continue that behavior, so only give him a treat if you really want him to continue a certain behavior.

If you like it, reward it!

Remember to reward the common, everyday behavior that you like, in addition to proper commands.

▲ *For example:* If you are in the kitchen and Fido is calmly lying down out of the way, then reward him. Toss him a little treat and say, "Good boy." Then continue what you were doing.

Rewarding doesn't need to be a big deal. Just communicate to Fido that you like the behavior. Many times owners don't reward Fido's good behavior because they don't notice it — but they do notice when Fido gets up from a calm position and begins to chew on the carpet. When Fido gets in trouble multiple times throughout the day, he gets discouraged because he is never rewarded for good behavior. He's only punished for the bad.

Whether it's during a training session or just around the house throughout the day, reward the behaviors you want to encourage.

21

4. Remove and replace

If Fido is doing something unacceptable, remove him from the environment, then give him a replacement activity.

▲ *For example:* If Fido is chewing on your toes, remove your toes from his mouth and give him a stuffed animal to chew instead.

When Fido gets older, the replacement can be a trained behavior. Consider a replacement for when he barks at the doorbell — you can teach him that the doorbell is his cue to go to his crate or to his bed. If this sounds like an impossible task, you can break it into puppy steps.

5. Puppy steps forward

Train everything in tiny increments, gradually introducing change and increasing the difficulty. By taking baby steps, you set your pup up for success and eliminate frustration during training for both of you.

6. Puppy steps back!

If Fido fails to obey for three consecutive attempts when training, return to the previous step and reteach him. No matter what the command or behavior is, reteach the previous step — and don't get frustrated.

⚠ *For example:* You've taught Fido to sit. Last training session, it seemed that he knew what to do, but now he just won't sit! What should you do? Go back a step — take a treat and lure him into the sit. Reward him. Now that he has had a refresher, get him in a new position and ask him to sit again, not luring him. Often Fido will remember how to sit and obey. If at this point he still doesn't sit, he does not thoroughly understand the command and you will need to practice more on the previous steps until he grasps the concept.

7. Short and frequent training

Training sessions for puppies should be 30 seconds to five minutes long. Aim for three to five short lessons per day. Puppies, like young kids, have short attention spans. Training for too long will create frustration for you and Fido.

Try to train just before Fido's meals; he will be motivated to train and be more focused on you and the reward. Keep sessions short and upbeat, and strive to end with a success.

8. Only give a command once

Repeating commands will teach the dog to ignore your requests.

Often, people fall into the habit of saying "Fido, Sit. Sit. Sit, Fido. Fido, Sit!" This teaches Fido that he doesn't need to listen the first eight times you give a command.

THERE ARE TWO MAIN REASONS THAT FIDO ISN'T LISTENING TO YOU:

1. He is distracted by something else.

He might hear you, but you aren't nearly as interesting as the distraction. In this instance, remove Fido from the distraction and try again. If removal is not possible (maybe you are out in a busy public area), then stop giving him the command. When you are away from distractions at a later time, ask for the behavior and gradually increase the distraction level so next time he will be able to handle the situation.

2. Fido just doesn't know the command yet.

Maybe you have taught it to him, but he hasn't fully grasped it. If so, then give him the command, but let him think for a few seconds. It's like when you take a test —

sometimes you just need to think about the question or problem for a few seconds (or even minutes) before you know the answer. Give your dog that time to think about what you are saying. Then, if he still doesn't show the correct behavior, reteach it, because it may jog his memory.

9. One command at one time

Resist the temptation to switch commands if Fido doesn't respond to your re-

24

quest. Give him one command and stay with it until he obeys or reteach it, or leave the subject until a later time.

Sometimes it's tempting to want Fido to just obey something, so you say, "Fido, sit. No, OK, well then down. Fido, down. C'mon! What about spin? Fido, spin!"

This totally confuses Fido! Which do you want him to do? He will quickly learn to not listen to your commands because you don't enforce any of them.

We say...

I'm really late for school Fido and it's going to take a long time to get ready. I've already been late once, Fido please hurry up and go to the bathroom!

10. He's smart, but not that smart.

Your dog is smart, but he can't understand paragraphs. Please don't speak to him in paragraphs.

Fido hears...

Laa la laaa laa Laaa la laa laaa Laa la laaa laa,...

"Fido, I'm really late for school and it's going to take a long time to heat up the car and get all my things together. I've already been late once this week, I really can't afford to be late again; my teacher was losing patience last time. So hurry up and go to the bathroom for me so I can get going!" Fido doesn't understand all that!

Just say, "Fido, go potty."

11. Being cute is not a trick!

Make him work for everything, even if it's just asking for a sit — always make him earn it. Incorporate training into daily routines, such as sit-stay before a meal, spin before going outside, etc. If he doesn't need to earn it, then he will prefer just lying around and having cookies come from the sky randomly. (I would like that too!)

If you ask Fido for a behavior and he doesn't obey, don't give him the treat, because he hasn't earned it. You can take a step backward and make it easier for him to obey, then reward him, but don't give him a treat unless he does what you've asked.

12. Praise

Praising your dog is very important. This involves scratching him behind the ears, often at his level, and telling him he's a good boy in a very happy voice. You must be genuinely happy about it. Dogs can tell if you are lying!

This lets Fido know you like what he did and it helps grow the bond between you. Praise is also important because when Fido gets older, you can praise him for something, and he won't always require a treat.

13. Consistency and expectations

If you set reasonable expectations and you are consistent, Fido will meet them. Many people just adapt to their dog's innate behaviors, and dismiss their own lack of training with "Fido just does that" or "He's rotten."

That is the lazy route. Fido's behaviors can be changed; you need to put in the effort and keep your expectations consistent. Dogs are intelligent animals that can meet high standards. It's OK to require Fido to be quiet when someone comes to the door. Choose how you want your dog to act and then baby step him into that behavior.

14. How to give commands

The tone of voice you use with Fido is very important. Dogs will react differently depending on the pitch of your voice. To demonstrate this, walk up to Fido and start talking quickly to him in a high-pitched voice, smiling and acting extremely happy. Fido's tail will probably thump on the ground, or he might walk up to see you, wagging his tail. Now, start talking to him in a very deep, slow voice. He will probably not be as excited, and he might even put his ears back and lower his tail because he thinks you are unhappy with him. Dogs react differently based on your tone of voice.

Some people envision giving commands to a dog as police officers command their dogs — in a deep, strong, forceful voice, almost yelling. On the other hand, first-time dog owners often give a command that sounds like a question or a request to obey.

2

These two methods will create drastically different dogs. When the command comes in too stern of a voice, the result is fear. The dog will most likely immediately obey you, but also might put his ears back in fear or nervousness. If you say the command in a tiny voice or as a question, Fido will probably ignore your command but will happily trot over to you looking for a pat on the head.

In general, commands should be given in an even tone, as if you are stating a fact. Say, "Fido, sit" in the same way you would say, "The sky is blue."

Exceptions:

1. Commands for puppies are given in a different manner than commands for adult dogs. For puppies, I always use a little bit of a higher pitch. I still say it as a fact, but a little softer and happier to keep the pup's attention and to make training fun in the pup's mind.

2. The one command that I do say differently, no matter the age of the dog, is "Come." I want this command to be an exciting and especially happy experience for Fido, no matter what. So, I always say it as if we are having a party as soon as he comes to me, because usually we do! I even do this with my older dogs because I want this to be more exciting and rewarding than any other command, for safety's sake.

29

15. Commands to use

You can use any command you want. I will give each behavior a name in this book, but you can use anything. If you would like Fido to sit when you say "orange," then just use the word orange when you are teaching him. The key is to have everyone in the family be consistent and use the same command when expecting a behavior.

Decide what words you are going to use as commands. The words you use to communicate his commands must be consistent. If you teach him the command "off" to mean get off the couch, everyone must use that command.

If some members of the household say "Down" to tell Fido to get off the couch and others use "off," Fido will get confused and not obey.

☞ Tricks are an opportunity to be creative with names of behaviors.

For example: You can teach Fido to play dead when you say the command, "Give me a kiss," as if Fido would rather die than kiss you.

16. Command sequence

"Fido's name, command"
"Marker," then reward.
"Release word"

▲ *For example*: "Fido, sit."
    "Yes." Give reward.

    "Break"

31

17. Patience

Perhaps the most necessary factor for dog training is patience. If you try to rush your dog, he will not enjoy training, may give up and then shut down. This will make you become frustrated with him and the lack of progress you are making. When dog training is no longer fun for you, then it becomes a chore. As a result, it will happen less often and Fido's behavior will go downhill. Make sure when you are training that you give your pup time to figure things out.

Dogs really do think! They are not programmable like a robot. If your training session isn't going well, stop and try again in a few hours when you can be patient and upbeat.

18. Trainer attitude

Dogs are very good at reading people; they can tell when you are upset or angry. Often your training reflects your mood. You need to be positive and relaxed to be patient with Fido. Training when you are in a rush or in a foul mood will create a situation where you get frustrated much faster than normal. Also, you will most likely not praise Fido as much for doing things correctly. Recognize your mood before you begin, then decide whether it is a good idea to train. It's okay to skip a day of training; training is not a race. It's much better to keep a good relationship with Fido and be a little behind schedule than to force training when it is not beneficial for either of you.

19. Negative and positive attention

In the past, training was almost exclusively negative, focusing on what Fido did wrong. Training has now swung the opposite direction, ignoring unwanted behaviors and rewarding desired ones.

Positive: With positive-only training, you completely ignore unwanted behaviors and reward the wanted ones. Training solely through positive reinforcement creates a dog willing to try different behaviors, guessing at what you want, which is good. The dogs use their brains, thinking about what they are doing, making many behaviors much quicker to teach.

Negative: Negative attention consists of marking and/or correcting unwanted behaviors. This fixes many behaviors quite quickly, but it also can create a dog with lower confidence and one who is not as willing to try to guess what you are wanting from him. I use very minimal corrections with puppies because they won't need anything more if their training begins at a young age. For me, minimal corrections means a corrective word/sound,

such as "No!" or "Ahh!" just to mark that the behavior they are doing is not acceptable. This is used for behaviors such as chewing on furniture, biting, relieving himself inside the house, etc. It marks that what the pup is doing right now is what I don't like and I'm going to give him an appropriate alternative (a chew toy, putting him outside to go to the bathroom, etc.).

With 8-10 week old puppies, I use positive attention 99% of the time. If a puppy jumps up, I ignore him until he sits, then reward with petting. But, some things need to be stopped immediately or are too rewarding for the puppy; in these instances I use small corrections. If you are in a situation where you can wait out bad behaviors, and they aren't self-rewarding for Fido, great! If not, it is OK to deliver corrections as long as they are given at the moment they are doing the wrong behavior, with the least amount of correction necessary, and with a calm attitude on your part.

20. Socialization

Socialization is the process of exposing your puppy to various objects, people, places and sounds, and teaching him to adapt in a way that builds confidence. Socialization should begin as soon as you get your pup, and continue until the pup is an adult.

Usually, the sooner you begin socialization, the more readily the pup will gain confidence and the more likely he will be to adapt to new situations as an adult.

To create a happy, well-behaved pet, socialization is necessary. If Fido is not properly socialized, he might be fearful or skittish of new objects and environments that he encounters. Some dogs might even react to new situations with aggression.

Whenever you are exposing Fido to something new, make it a positive and fun experience for him. I take my new puppies into big box hardware stores or feed stores the first week I have them. While they are there, they get many treats and we let nice strangers pet them to build up their confidence in people and new areas.

If there is an item that is "scary" and upsetting to Fido (mailboxes, large garbage cans or various other objects and occurrences), perform a "Jolly routine" — going up to the "scary" object, laughing and having a conversation with it. Don't force Fido to come any closer to the object than he feels comfortable. As you laugh and talk to the scary object, Fido will become curious and start to investigate since you have indicated you don't see it as a threat. Let Fido approach the new object on his own terms and at his own speed. Do not pull him towards it, as this will have the opposite effect and cause him to fear everything new.

Feel free to give him treats when approaching the object or person to associate the new experience with pleasure and get his mind off the object.

For a list of things to expose Fido to, see page 169.

Chapter 3

Starting on the Right Paw

Respect

Dogs need to be treated with respect. If you don't respect them, they won't respect you. Don't overpower them, don't treat them like babies, and give them their space.

Sometimes a person — or a dog — just needs to be alone. A dog's crate is his room. If Fido goes into his crate voluntarily at any point, *never* disturb him. He is saying, "I'm tired. I need some calm, and I don't want to be bothered." This is healthy; everyone needs a break at times.

Young children often have a hard time understanding that dogs aren't like stuffed animals that they can play with however they like. This can cause problems in the household. They need to be taught to be patient and that the dog needs to be treated kindly and left alone when he is in his crate. In an hour or two he will want to play again.

One scenario that I have seen repeatedly with young children is a game of chase, or "keep away." It often evolves unintentionally, but this is perhaps the worst interaction to have with Fido.

IT TYPICALLY HAPPENS LIKE THIS:

A little girl, Susie, is playing fetch with Fido — great! The game gets a little boring, so she picks up the toy and decides to put it behind her back so Fido can't see it. Fido wonders why the game stopped, so he tries to go behind Susie to find the toy. Susie then turns around so Fido can't find the toy, and she is now walking quickly backward with Fido following. This is a fun game for Susie and she starts getting a little excited, walking away faster from her dog and squealing with excitement because it's so fun.

But Fido feeds off that excitement and forgets his manners. Fido begins to jump up a little, exciting Susie, which excites Fido, which excites Susie, etc., until Susie actually gets scared — but Fido is still playing.

Now Susie starts trying to get away from Fido out of fear and when she can't, she holds the toy above her head to protect her hands and to keep Fido from getting it. But Fido is in such an aroused state that he jumps to try to get it, scaring Susie even more. Susie lowers the toy at some point and Fido jumps to get it and accidentally bites Susie's hand. She is now crying and terrified, runs to a parent and says the dog bit her. Fido is confused because he is in big trouble — and he was just playing! This situation can even escalate to Fido being re-homed because the children are scared of him.

Be sure every interaction with Fido is beneficial and respectful.

Who's in charge?

Dogs are pack animals, so they are going to look at one person in the family as the leader. Even if you want Fido to be a family dog, he will still view one specific person as "in charge." Dogs will give attention to everyone, but when Fido is hungry or wants to go outside, he will often go to the one he sees as "the top dog." Usually this person is the one who feeds, walks and trains him — the one that cares for his needs. So what does this mean? Decide from the first day whose dog Fido is. If it is a child's dog, then the child needs to be the one to do 90 percent of the work.

I was worried about this when I got my Border Collie, Elliott. Border Collies become obsessive about everything, especially the person that they work for — they are "one-person" dogs. I really didn't want Elliott to become attached to my mom, and I knew this was a possibility because I was gone at school all day and he would be with her.

So for the first six months of his life, I asked my mom to not give him much attention at all, and I was the one who always fed him, played with him and trained him. Sometimes, I even asked my parents to stop petting him or playing fetch with him because I wanted to be sure that he wouldn't become attached. I probably went a little overboard with this, and it was a little hard on my mom, but he is definitely "my" dog. Anyone is allowed to play with him now, and he loves everyone. He will go around asking everyone to play fetch with him at some point, but he works for me the most.

Before bringing your dog home, determine whose dog it's going to be. That person needs to do the work. You don't have to go to the extreme as I did, but a child in charge will need to do more work to become the one in charge, rather than the father or mother.

If it is going to be the children's dog and more than one child will be in charge, they will all need to pitch in and take care of him.

Nothing in life is free (NILIF)

The purpose of NILIF is to teach Fido that all good things come from you, and he must earn what he wants. This is not mandatory, but is recommended for the first few weeks Fido comes to your home because it creates a mentality that will last for his lifetime. Usually, I keep NILIF in place strictly for two weeks, then gradually phase out some parts.

Throughout my dogs' lives, though, they always have to work for certain things, such as staying in a sit before dinner and sitting before being let outside.

The owner must not give away anything for free — whether it's a pat on the head, playing fetch with a toy, or giving him a treat or a meal. Before your dog gets anything, he must obey a command.

BELOW ARE A FEW EXAMPLES:

Walks: Before going on a walk, have Fido sit at the door. Then put the leash on. Open the door only when he is sitting calmly. Be patient — just wait if he is wound up. Eventually he will sit. Then open the door and release him to go out.

Meals: For the first two weeks, puppies get all their meals through training. Instead of treats I use two to three kibbles. After each meal/training, I put the rest of his meal down to ensure he is eating the correct amount. After two or three weeks of hand feeding/training then you can just put Fido in a sit or down stay and set down his bowl. Wait approximately five seconds, then give his release word so he can eat.

Fetch: Throw a toy for Fido. When he returns, ask him to perform a task – sit, down, spin, beg, sit pretty, etc. After he obeys, throw the toy again.

This technique reminds Fido he must do what you want before he gets what he wants. It continues to demonstrate your leadership and sets rules in the household. This is a great way to practice commands daily as well, because the dog is happy to do it since he wants to work and wants the reward. The exception to NILIF if you would like to do something to show your affection, then Fido doesn't have to work for it.

▲ *For example:* If you would like to pet Fido, but he is not asking for it, then you don't need to require Fido to respond to a command. But, if a few minutes later Fido comes to you and puts his nose under your arm asking to be petted, then give him a command, and as a reward for obeying, pet him.

Manners

Staying off furniture: Before you get Fido, thoroughly think through (and agree, if you are a family) whether you want to allow him on furniture. My dogs aren't allowed on any furniture except my bed; this is a personal preference because I don't want them getting the couch dirty and jumping up when guests are visiting. Also, it establishes that it is my furniture, and they do not become possessive of it.

☛ If you are OK with Fido on the furniture, ensure Fido only gets on when invited. Otherwise he may become possessive.

One client I had asked how to stop his dog from biting. After a few questions, I discovered the dog only bit when he was on furniture — a classic sign of possessiveness. A dog is less likely to become possessive if you only allow him to get on after he performs a behavior (NILIF technique).

To keep Fido off furniture entirely, I start training as soon as he comes home. If Fido puts his paws up on the furniture, immediately withdraw your hands so you are not making any contact, then ask for a sit. If he sits, get down on the ground with him and reward him with praise. If you ask for a sit two times and he doesn't listen or get off, then push him off firmly. If he puts his paws up again, repeat. The key is to be sure every family member is doing this; if just one person allows the pup on the furniture, Fido may never learn.

Jumping up: All dogs jump on people if not taught otherwise. It's their way of showing they want attention. It's easiest to stop this behavior if you begin training the

minute you bring Fido home. Because the motivation for jumping is attention, the solution is to not give any attention until the puppy does something you like, e.g. sit. I ignore puppies until they stop jumping and sit. When I first get a pup, I begin to teach sit during training. In addition, I immediately ignore the puppy whenever he or she jumps on me. Because puppies are learning that a sit gets a reward, they will begin to sit outside of training sessions, in hopes of getting a treat.

So when you ignore them for jumping up, they will usually sit since it's the only behavior they are confident will get rewarded. When they do sit, crouch down and praise! Be sure every person in the household only interacts with Fido when he has four paws on the floor.

Biting

Biting is something everyone expects from a puppy, but it still hurts. Because of this, it's important to stop it as soon as possible so you and your pup can have a good relationship.

THERE ARE A FEW REASONS WHY PUPS WILL BITE:

Play: When puppies play they bite, tackle, and jump on each other. Puppies must learn the appropriate way to play with humans. When Fido first comes home to you, he will not understand that he cannot interact with you as he did with his siblings.

Teething: When puppies go through the teething stage, they are more prone to chewing on your fingers because it feels good to them.

If Fido is biting because he is playing or teething

Option 1: Say, "Ouch!" loudly in a high-pitched voice when his teeth touch your skin — even if it doesn't hurt, and freeze for five seconds. Then you may continue playing with Fido. After you have had to yell "Ouch!" three times, put Fido away — in his crate or on a leash without interaction from you. Then in 5 minutes or so, try to play with him again.

44

Option 2: When Fido's teeth touch your skin, say "Ouch" (Option 1), but add a negative association with biting you. Since Fido is biting your fingers already, just hold his lower jaw — one finger on the inside of his mouth pressing down and one on the outside underneath, pressing up. Hold it firmly for approximately three seconds. Fido will be uncomfortable and may try to squirm away, but keep hold until three seconds are up. Repeat this each time he bites your fingers. If after a few repetitions it hasn't discouraged him, hold more firmly, so that it is a little more uncomfortable.

Option 2 is cause and effect — pup bites then pup feels discomfort. If this is done from the very beginning, the pup will know within a few days to not bite. It is especially important to stop biting immediately in a family with children, as puppies find that children are the most fun to gnaw on because the children squeal and seem to immediately want to play a game of chase when bitten – How fun! This starts for a very bad relationship between the child and dog.

Aggression: A third reason Fido may bite is if he has a bone or another highly valued object — then it is most likely a result of aggression and possessiveness. This needs to be stopped immediately. Go to the resource guarding section to see how to stop it (page 154).

As with everything, teach Fido to not bite by starting very softly, and only increasing the intensity of the correction gradually and as needed.

Showing affection

Animals are all different in the way they communicate and show affection. Even within a species, each animal has a different personality and enjoys different activities. Humans show affection by touch and through speech, but this is not how dogs show affection. You must speak "in his language" in order for you and your dog to have the best relationship. Most dogs don't enjoy hugging; it confines them and can appear that you are trying to show dominance, making them uncomfortable.

So, how do you show affection then? Each dog is different. My Corgi loves belly rubs — if I start petting her on the head, she will immediately roll over onto her back and wiggle her legs, saying, "Pet my belly!" My Border Collie doesn't enjoy petting; all he wants is to play fetch. If I start to pet him, he will run off and return with a toy or sock for me to throw. My dogs have completely different love languages, and I need to understand this and work with it. If I were to only pet my Border Collie to show affection, he would be very unhappy. But, because my love language is petting, I will occasionally tell him to sit in my lap for a minute or two so I can pet him, and he will put up with it.

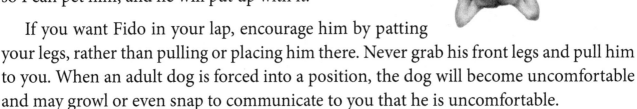

If you want Fido in your lap, encourage him by patting your legs, rather than pulling or placing him there. Never grab his front legs and pull him to you. When an adult dog is forced into a position, the dog will become uncomfortable and may growl or even snap to communicate to you that he is uncomfortable.

Introducing the puppy to other animals that live in your home

Dogs: I've had approximately 40 puppies come through my household over the past four years, and my three permanent, older dogs have had to adjust to each one. This is what I've found:

- None of the dogs became friends with a puppy immediately.
- The older dogs growled, bared their teeth and moved away when the pup interacted, at first.
- The older dogs never hurt a puppy, no matter how annoyed.
- Supervise all interactions between the dog and pup when the pup comes home.

Puppies jump on each other's heads to initiate a game of wrestling, so they do not know social boundaries. The older dogs will not put up with this, and it's their job to teach boundaries.

If the older dog gets too forceful or irritated with the pup, calmly remove the puppy from the situation. Exercise pens or baby gates can be used to let the puppy be near the older dog, but still give both dogs space.

Usually the dog and puppy will work it out, after some time, but always be close by in case they need separating.

Cats: Cats are a little more difficult to introduce a puppy to. A cat's initial response is to run to a high place and stare at the new puppy. Unfortunately, in the act of running away, cats are initiating a game of chase in the eyes of the puppy.

If the puppy is allowed to chase the cat during that first interaction, your life will become a lot more difficult. If you have a cat, then don't let the pup interact with the cat off-leash for the first few weeks.

Let them get accustomed to each other when the puppy is on a leash, and give a quick verbal correction as well as a small correction with the leash ("Ahhh" and a short jerk) if the pup ever tries to chase the cat.

If the cat stands looking at your pup, and the pup slowly goes over to investigate, allow them to meet. Often the cat will give a swift bat to the pup's nose. This is perfectly fine, and teaches the pup to stay away from the cat without you needing to interfere. Sometimes the cat likes the pup and will rub on him, initiating a friendship.

Overall, keep the pup on a leash and away from the cat until you have observed multiple acceptable interactions.

Other animals: The best time to show a puppy other small animals is when the pup is tired from exercise, just waking up from a nap or beginning to doze off. This way, the pup won't be very interested.

If he is shown these animals three or four times when he is sleepy, he will become accustomed to them but not care, which is the perfect relationship.

Chapter 4

Living with Your Dog

Housebreaking

The best way to housetrain a dog is to not let him go to the bathroom inside. (Ha! That's a joke, right?) Yes, but, really, taking him out often and keeping him on a schedule ensures he rarely has an accident in the house, and teaches him outside is the place to relieve himself. The key here is to have your pup on a regular exercise, sleep and feeding schedule. What goes in on a schedule comes out on a schedule!

Fido needs to be crate-trained so he will be comfortable taking naps and going to bed in the crate. The crate should be an area small enough that Fido won't relieve himself in it. A good rule of thumb is to have the crate 1 1/3 the pup's height and length. Crate training lets you take a break from monitoring the pup without ruining any house-training progress.

Always supervise your pup. Fido should never be alone unless he is in his crate. When I don't want Fido to be in his crate, I put him on a leash beside me; whether it is in the kitchen eating dinner, in the living room reading or in the basement watching TV, he is always on a leash next to me. It's not a retractable leash, just a 4- to 6-foot regular leash and a buckle collar. This keeps Fido from sneaking off and relieving himself away from me, and I will not be unpleasantly surprised by a present that he has so graciously left me.

Because Fido will be within a 6-foot radius of me, I can watch his body language to know when he needs to go outside.

YOUR DOG WILL NEED TO BE TAKEN OUTSIDE AT THE FOLLOWING TIMES:

- 15 to 30 minutes after a meal

- Immediately after being taken out of the crate

- Immediately after waking up

- When he stops playing and looks around

- Any time you are interacting and he begins sniffing the ground

- Any time you are interacting and he leaves to go to another room

- When he suddenly grows more hyper than usual

Sometimes this seems constant! An 8-week-old pup, when not in his crate, needs to go out about every hour to prevent accidents, sometimes more. But with time, Fido will be able to "hold it" longer, and you will learn his body language that signals he needs to go outside.

Where should the crate go? The placement of a crate is very important. If it is in a busy area, the pup will never sleep. If it is in the garage or basement, the pup will feel like he is not part of the "pack" and will cry/bark because he is alone. The crate placement is based on how often your family is in each room. If your family is always in the living room, don't put the pup's crate there; put it in a room next to the living room or two rooms away. Placing it too far away will make him feel separate from the family and will increase his energy level when he is let out because he will be so excited.

I worked with one family where the dog's crate was in the basement, in the workout room, with the doors shut. When let out of the crate, the dog was so excited that he would "leak" because he couldn't contain his joy, so they had to immediately take him outside. The dog felt like he was banished when he was in his crate, and it became like a punishment for him.

The crate should be in a room where the pup won't be disturbed by people walking past and talking loudly, but he can still hear the family.

I recommend putting the crate next to the main caretaker's bed. This way Fido can hear and smell someone at night, but during the day — when he is taking naps — he is away from the noise and sounds of the family.

53

What about at night? Ideally, the breeder has already gotten Fido accustomed to the crate by letting him sleep inside it (maybe with siblings) for a few nights before you brought him home. If this is the case, then you can start crate training and have him in the crate at night without too much of a fuss.

If this is not the case, begin the first few steps of crate training (page 73) during the day so he will get a little more comfortable in it before he goes in for the night. When you put him away for bedtime, give him two or three high-value rewards and prepare for a noisy night. It goes more smoothly if he has a blanket (not a bed yet) and a stuffed animal in the crate with him so he has something to cuddle up against (like his siblings). Sometimes putting a blanket over his crate can also help him settle. Then just wait for him to fall asleep.

Potty: If Fido is younger than 10 weeks old, he will likely need to relieve himself in the middle of the night. If his crate is the correct size, he will begin crying because he doesn't want to foul his "den." When he cries, take him outside, but do not talk to him or cuddle him; you don't want to make these trips particularly enjoyable, or Fido will learn it's fun to wake up at night and will develop a habit. The goal is to phase out the nighttime bathroom breaks ASAP. (Trust me, you will want to phase these out after getting up several nights in a row!) Put a leash on Fido, set him on the grass and slowly walk around, letting

54

him sniff. If he needs to go, he will go within 60 seconds or so. If he loses interest, take him inside. This is all done without talking, cuddling or petting — it's a business trip.

If the need to go out at night persists for more than two weeks try moving the dinner feeding to a slightly earlier time or limiting the amount of water within a few hours of bedtime. Or, begin to schedule the middle-of-the-night "go out" time when the dog has been needing to go out, and then gradually move the time you take him out by half-hour or hour increments toward morning. Be sure to discuss it with your veterinarian in case Fido has a medical issue. The longest it has ever taken one of my pups to sleep through the night is two weeks.

Crying: If Fido is making noise in his crate and you know he isn't hungry, thirsty, or needs to relieve himself, the best thing to do is ignore him. Most pups will eventually stop crying with the combination of being ignored and daytime crate training.

Housebreaking progression: As Fido gets older, I gradually give him more freedom. When he is doing well, I can let him stay in a small room with a baby gate, then a few weeks later he can stay in two rooms, etc. This way Fido gains independence and freedom at the same pace he gains control over his bodily functions. Be careful not to give too much freedom too soon.

A TYPICAL PUPPY IN TRAINING WITH ME HAS THE FOLLOWING NUMBER OF ACCIDENTS:

- 8 to 10 weeks old: Three accidents per week
- 11 to 12 weeks old: Two accidents per week
- 12 to 14 weeks old: One accident per week
- 14 weeks to 6 months old: Maybe two or three accidents total

Now, this looks pretty impressive — 14 accidents in the house throughout the puppy's life. This is not because I have the dog trained at 8 weeks; it's because I am extremely careful to minimize the amount of times the pup can make a mistake. This is up to the owner. The fewer mistakes you allow the dog to have, the faster he will learn. If I train more than one pup at a time, often I get careless and the pups make many more mistakes. I then blame myself rather than the pups because it's my job to keep a closer eye on them.

When Fido does make a mistake: If I catch him in the act, I say "No" firmly and pick him up. Hopefully this stops the 'flow,' then I take him outside for him to continue. I praise him when he goes in the correct area, saying "Good go potty!" in a happy voice. This is to let him know he isn't in trouble for relieving himself; he is just supposed to do it in the designated area.

When you find a present Fido has previously left: Clean it up with disinfectant, making sure to get the smell out. Otherwise, he will be encouraged to continue to go in that spot. Don't punish Fido, because he will not understand the reason for the punishment.

Keeping the yard clean: To keep the yard clean, I teach the pups to relieve themselves in a certain area of the yard. There is an area where we don't mow the grass, and I teach all the pups to go there. The long grass shows the pups the boundaries of the area, and it is easy for us to remember to be careful of the "landmines" there.

This is taught the same way as the rest of housebreaking — by only letting Fido go to potty in that specific area. For the first two weeks, I carry Fido out to that area and wait for him to relieve himself there, then praise. Then, for three weeks I walk him over to that area and praise when he relieves himself.

By the end of training, most pups have learned to go to the designated area to relieve themselves without me accompanying them. If you have observed Fido not going to that area, then continue walking him to the area until he understands. If Fido makes a mistake and doesn't relieve himself in the designated area, do not reprimand him. Just return to walking him to the designated area.

Physical exercise

All dogs need physical exercise to live happy and healthy lives. Different breeds and temperaments will need different amounts of exercise, but whether a Chihuahua or a Saint Bernard, they all need exercise. There are many ways to exercise a dog, with the most common being walking or jogging. However, some people don't have a place to walk their dog safely, or Fido is so energetic that the owner isn't capable of maintaining a speed that would actually wear Fido out.

LISTED BELOW ARE SOME ALTERNATIVES:

Fetch: Some breeds, such as retrievers, love to play fetch and will play for hours. Fetch is helpful for exercising large breeds with lots of energy because all you have to do is throw the ball, disc or other toy. Dogs that truly love fetch will tire out more quickly playing than just running.

Tug O' War: This is a great game to play with your dog if you and Fido know the boundaries. Before you play this game, you need to establish the rules. To learn how to correctly play tug o' war, go to page 119. If done correctly, this game can help build your relationship because you are the key to a fun game.

Agility: Dog agility is a sport consisting of an obstacle course for your dog. It can be a great way to exercise Fido while getting him focused and obeying you. It tires Fido out quickly, as he must go over jumps, up ramps, etc. If you have a large yard, I highly recommend this. There are competitions and a tight-knit group of sportsmen in most areas of the country.

Swimming: If it's available in your area, swimming is a terrific exercise for dogs. It wears them out quickly because of the effort required, and most dogs love it! You can play fetch with your dog by throwing a toy into the water and asking him to retrieve it.

However, some dogs don't enjoy water. If this is the case, don't force Fido to swim. Never push him in because that will create a fear of water — exactly what you don't want. Let Fido go in at his own pace.

An effective way to get him to try out the water independently is to have another dog that enjoys the water play fetch into the water with your dog nearby. If they are both off-leash, then often the dog not comfortable with water will try it out because he wants to join in the excitement.

Treadmill: Training Fido to run on a treadmill is a great way to exercise him on rainy or snowy days, or if you are not capable of tiring him out yourself. Even with treadmill time, Fido still needs a leisurely walk outside each day to smell different things and get out of the house.

 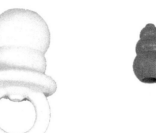 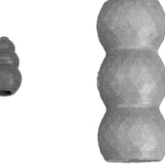 

Various Kong® toys

Mental exercise

Dogs need physical exercise, but they also need mental exercise. We sometimes forget that we need to give our dogs something that will entertain and build their brains. If dogs aren't given something to do, bad behaviors like chewing shoes or furniture, digging and barking can form quickly.

Mental exercise will also help dogs be less restless and energetic. I imagine that I would be restless too if I was forced to sleep or stare at the wall all day, every day. People play games, talk to friends, go to school or work, read books, watch movies, go out to eat, etc. We have lots of ways to entertain ourselves, and pay money just for the privilege. Dogs don't have this capability, so we need to do it for them.

HERE ARE SOME WAYS TO EXERCISE YOUR DOG MENTALLY:

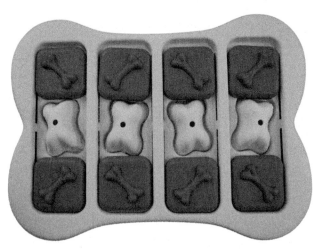

Dog puzzles: These puzzles are created specifically for dogs. You place treats in all of the compartments, and your dog must use his nose or paws to move the pieces to get the treats. These puzzles help the dog learn persistence and make him think.

Work to eat toys: One of the most popular dog toy brands is Kong®. Their original toy is another type of dog puzzle. Peanut butter or some other type of food reward is put inside the rubber toy, and the dog licks it, trying to get the reward. This occupies dogs for a long time and is very useful, especially to keep puppies out of trouble! Freezing the toy with peanut butter in the compartment keeps them engaged even longer.

Training: Teaching Fido a new behavior is a great way to stimulate his brain while building a good relationship. Try teaching Fido tricks to keep training fun and fresh for you. To see a selection of tricks and their instructions, go to page 106.

TV: Some dogs actually watch TV. One of my dogs runs and sits in front of the screen after dinner. When the weather is bad, he will sometimes get to watch a movie. If the TV excites your dog, be sure the TV is high enough to prevent him from injuring himself (or the TV).

4

Chapter 5

Nuts and Bolts of Training

Three methods of training

Training is teaching a dog to repeat an action when requested. There are three methodologies for training — forcing, luring, and shaping.

This book primarily uses the luring method because it is simpler for the trainer to understand, and the dog enjoys the training. Some behaviors, however, will be taught through shaping, depending on the complexity of the end behavior.

1. **Forcing** — requires physically maneuvering the dog into the desired position. This method is somewhat stressful to the dog and not very effective, so I do not recommend it.

   ▲ *For example:* If a trainer is teaching sit, he will pull up on the collar and push down on the dog's rear.

2. **Luring** — The trainer moves an object that the dog values in a way that results in the dog unconsciously performing the correct actions.

▲ *For example:* To teach sit, the trainer holds a treat in his hand and after Fido nibbles on it, the trainer will then bring the treat up and back so Fido's head goes backwards and the dog's rear goes to the ground.

3. **Shaping** — rewarding the dog as he gets closer to performing the desired behavior.

Shaping has become a more common training method. The idea behind shaping is to allow the dog to participate in learning by letting him think about what he is doing and what he wants.

This method rewards a dog as it gets closer and closer to the desired behavior — much like the hot and cold game. The section on Crate Training (page 73) is a description of shaping the dog to happily get into its crate. Trainers often use this method with a clicker, or sometimes a marker word such as "yes" is used (see more about this on pages 68-70).

▲ *For example:* To teach Fido to sit on a box, the trainer will set a box on the ground and reward Fido every time he looked at the box. Then the trainer will reward when Fido steps closer to the box, sniffs the box, touches the box with his paw, puts a paw on the box, etc., until Fido climbs on top of the box.

Rewards

Dogs, like people, have independent likes and dislikes. My Border Collie doesn't care much about food, but will do anything for a game of tug o' war or fetch. On the other hand, my Corgi will jump over the moon for a piece of hot dog!

The purpose of treats is to encourage a behavior, not to fill up a dog. To keep Fido on a healthy diet where treats do not replace his normal food, the treats should be very small, i.e. the size of a chocolate chip. This is big enough for Fido to enjoy it and want more, but small enough that he doesn't become full.

Almost all dogs will work for food, but treats might need to be tastier for a less food-motivated dog. Most behaviors are easiest to train with treats rather than toys, so determine what treats your dog will work for. It is possible to use toys of different values, but you might need to adjust instructions. There are also real-life rewards — such as fetch, tug, going for a walk, going outside, eating dinner, agility, belly rub, etc.

SUGGESTED TREAT VALUES

Good = Carrots
- Kibble
- Milkbones™
- Treats with flour or meal as the first ingredient

Better = Chips
- Treats with meat as the first ingredient
- Cheese

Best = Ice Cream
- Hot dogs
- Beef
- Chicken
- Liver

5

Fido's first vocabulary

1. Positive marker: "Good job, Fido, I'm going to reward you." The positive marker should be said (or clicked if using clicker training — see page 70) as soon as Fido performs the correct behavior. Then he should be given a treat immediately.

This should be said neutrally, not too excitedly nor sternly. Examples of positive marker words: "Yes," "Good," "Great," "Yup," or you can also use a clicker (which I will cover a bit further in this chapter).

Teaching Fido the marker word

Treats: Better

1. Say your marker word or click the clicker.

2. Immediately reward.

3. Repeat when Fido is in different places, situations, etc. *About 40 repetitions.*

Give Fido the reward as soon as possible.

After Fido knows what the marker word or sound means, then it will be OK later on if you are occasionally delayed in giving him a treat because you have marked the behavior and communicated that the treat is coming.

2. Negative marker: "That's not quite what I'm wanting, but keep trying." A negative marker is not a word used to punish Fido; it's a word to communicate that what he is doing is not going to get him a reward.

I don't recommend using "no" because it is too easy to slip into saying it as if Fido is in trouble, rather than as a form of marking. It is not used the same way as "Ahhh." "Ahhh" is used to stop a behavior and communicate that it is bad, while a negative marker word simply communicates that the behavior is not what you are looking for and it is used during a training session.

The negative marker should be said neutrally — not excitedly, nor sternly. Examples of negative marker words: "Oops," "Uh-oh," "Whoops."

Use this word when you are training Fido to exhibit a specific behavior and he performs one that you are not looking for. If you are teaching Fido to lie down and he stands up, say "Oops" (or your negative marker) and retry it.

Fido will learn what this means through repetition. It does not need to be taught like the positive marker.

3. Release word: Signals to Fido that he can be done with that specific behavior and can get out of position. After each command, Fido should hear his release word. This should be said excitedly to communicate that he can break position. Examples of release words: "Break," "Free," and "OK!"

The release word is especially important to use for stays, to signal that Fido can move and the exercise is over.

Clicker training

Clicker training is a type of positive reinforcement training that uses a specific sound, made from a plastic or metal device, called a "clicker," to communicate to the dog and encourage a specific behavior. The use of the clicker was conceived in the 1940s with the theory that animals were not receiving clear communication through voice and that a clear-sounding marker, prior to some type of treat, would shorten training time. In the 1990s, clicker training for dogs gained popularity.

When clicker training, the behavior is taught prior to the command being added. This means that you catch or shape Fido into the desired position, and as soon as he is in the position, he hears the click and is then given a reward. Fido learns to think about what he is doing when he hears the click, so he is able to repeat it and get another reward.

Throughout this book, M/R means "Mark and Reward". Which is itself short for mark the moment/reward the behavior. M/R can take many forms such as a click of your clicker followed by a treat, or "Yes" followed by a game of tug. For most dogs, treats are most effective, but each dog is different.

While clickers are undoubtedly effective in training, they do have some drawbacks. They are not always with you, and a clicker can be cumbersome to use with a leash and treats.

I use marker words for the majority of training, as they don't require anything except voice. However, if you are interested in teaching complicated tricks or competition-level obedience, then the clicker might be the best tool, as it is a little more accurate than using a marker word.

Chapter 6

- Crate training
- Name game
- Watch me
- Sit
- Come
- Down
- Stand
- Heel
- Leash training
- Sit-stay
- Down-stay

Basic Lessons

Throughout this book, M/R means "Mark and Reward". Which is itself short for mark the moment/reward the behavior. M/R can take many forms such as a click of your clicker followed by a treat, or "Yes" followed by a game of tug. For most dogs, treats are most effective, but each dog is different.

CRATE TRAINING

Reward value: Best

Difficulty: Medium

Make sure you: Begin crate training as soon as you get Fido — as in that day. Remember to keep sessions short and upbeat with lots of praise. Five minutes maximum.

Begin with the crate door open, without any bed or blanket on the bottom. Sit or kneel near the crate and let Fido walk freely in the room.

❶ When Fido acknowledges the crate (sniffs it, looks at it, etc.), **M/R**. *About 3 repetitions.*

❷ When Fido takes one step towards the crate, **M/R**. Don't lure him; be patient! *About 3 repetitions.*

❸ When Fido takes two steps towards the crate, **M/R**. *About 3 repetitions.*

❹ When Fido puts his head inside the crate, **M/R**. *About 2 repetitions.*

❺ When Fido places one paw inside the crate, **M/R**. *About 3 repetitions.*

❻ Repeat Step 5 for two paws, three paws, and then four paws.

❼ Wait for Fido to go in the crate. Reward. Wait for him to come back out, and when he does, ignore him. If he chooses to go back in the crate, reward three times and praise. *About 10 repetitions.*

Wait for Fido to go in the crate

Reward in the top back corner of the crate

Wait for him to come back out, then ignore him

If he chooses to go back in

Reward 3 times and praise

❽ Open the door and wait for Fido to choose to go in. When Fido goes in the crate, reward three times in the top back corner of the crate through the wires, then give his release word. *About 5 repetitions.*

Wait for Fido to go in crate   *Reward 3 times and praise*   *Give Fido's release word*

❾ When Fido goes in the crate voluntarily, close and latch the door, reward in the back corner of the crate 3 times, open the door, and give Fido's release word.
About 10 repetitions.

When Fido goes in, close and latch door   *Reward 3 times*   *Open door*   *Give Fido's release word*

❿ When Fido goes in the crate voluntarily, reward once in the top back corner of the crate without closing the door. Wait for Fido to try to leave the crate. When he does, close the door quickly before he can get out. Keep the door shut until Fido sits voluntarily. If he gets up, shut the door again and wait for him to sit voluntarily again. Then give Fido the release word and reward him when he comes out of the crate. Repeat until you can leave the door open for a few seconds without him moving positions, then give Fido's release word and reward him. *About 10 repetitions.*

When Fido enters crate, reward

Wait for Fido to try to leave crate

When he tries to leave, quickly close door

Keep door shut until he sits

When he sits, open door

If he doesn't try to leave, give his release word

Reward and praise!

⓫ Begin leaving the room for short periods of time (at first leaving and coming back immediately). When you return, open the crate, reward in the crate, and then give his release word. Do not make your return an event, or Fido might be so anxious for you to return that he begins to have separation anxiety.

Note: *If Fido never steps toward the crate or goes in, then you can lure him by throwing treats or just taking a treat in your hand and putting it at the back of the cage. However, waiting patiently for him to choose to go in is a better training method that will make for a more completely learned lesson and a happier pup.*

Benefits of crate training:
- Gives you a break: No matter how cute Fido is, you will need a break!
- Prevents accidents: If sized properly, Fido won't soil his crate.
- Prevents separation anxiety: It gives Fido a safe, consistent place to stay.
- Protects your house: It keeps Fido away from everything destructible.

76

> **NAME GAME** (teaches your puppy his name)
>
> **Reward value:** Better
>
> **Difficulty:** Easy
>
> **Make sure you:** Begin with no distractions.

1 Say Fido's name in a happy, excited voice and reward him — whether he acknowledges you or not. *About 20 repetitions.*

Say Fido's name and present reward

Give reward

2 Say Fido's name in a happy voice and when he looks toward you, **M/R**. *About 20 repetitions.*

Say Fido's name and wait until he looks toward you

When he looks, M/R

77

❸ Say Fido's name in a happy voice and when he makes eye contact, **M/R**. *About 20 repetitions.*

Say Fido's name and wait until he makes eye contact with you

When he makes eye contact, M/R.

❹ Repeat Step 2 in gradually more distracting environments.

After Fido learns his name, always use the name accompanied with a command — never just his name when you want or need him to do something. Many owners say "Fido! Fido! Fido! Fido," and then get frustrated that Fido isn't responding. That's because they never say a command. As a result, Fido has learned to tune them out because they aren't saying anything that matters to him. You should be saying, "Fido, come," "Fido, sit," etc. After he learns his name, only say "Fido, (command)."

> **WATCH ME**
>
> **Reward value:** Better
>
> **Difficulty:** Easy
>
> **Make sure you:** Begin without any distractions present.

The purpose of Watch Me is to teach your dog to make eye contact with you so you have his attention. This is useful if there is a distraction and you want to give Fido a command, but he isn't paying attention to you. It can also be a training tool for distractions if your dog is reactive towards other dogs or animals.

Method 1

❶ Hold a reward under your chin. When Fido looks toward your face, **M/R**. *About 10 repetitions.*

Hold a reward under your chin   *M/R when Fido looks toward your face*

❷ Hold a reward under your chin. When Fido makes eye contact with you, **M/R**. *About 10 repetitions.*

❸ Say the cue for Watch Me, hold the reward under your chin. When Fido makes eye contact, **M/R**. *About 10 repetitions.*

79

❹ Without a treat, but as if you had one, say the cue and move your hand to your chin. When he makes eye contact with you, **M/R**. *About 20 repetitions.*

❺ Say the cue, but do not move your hand. When Fido makes eye contact, **M/R**.

Method 2

Get Fido interested in a reward (don't give it to him)

Put both hands behind your back

Wait for Fido to look at your face

M/R when he looks at your face

❶ Get Fido interested in a reward in your hand, then put both hands behind your back so Fido can't see the reward or your hands. When Fido looks up at your face, **M/R**. *About 10 repetitions.*

❷ Get Fido interested in the reward, then put both hands behind your back so Fido can't see the reward or your hands. When Fido makes eye contact, **M/R**. *About 10 repetitions.*

❸ Say the cue for Watch Me. Repeat Step 2, and **M/R** when Fido makes eye contact. *About 10 repetitions.*

❹ Say the cue for Watch Me, but do not move your hands behind your back — wait for Fido to make eye contact, then **M/R**. *About 10 repetitions.*

SIT

Reward value: Better

Difficulty: Easy

❶ Hold the treat between you forefinger and thumb. Let Fido nibble it for two seconds, then slowly move it upward and backward from his nose in an arc towards his tail. He will look up at the treat and consequently lower his rump. When his rump is on the ground, **M/R** with the treat in your hand. *About 20 repetitions.*

Let Fido nibble treat between your fingers

Slowly move the treat upward and backward

Continue gradually moving treat as Fido nibbles

When his rump is on the ground, M/R

❷ As you lure Fido into the sit position (Step 1), say the word "Sit." *About 10 repetitions.*

❸ Say "Fido, sit" and repeat the hand motion as if you were luring Fido, but without a treat in your hand. When he sits, **M/R**. *About 20 repetitions.*

4 Gradually morph the luring hand motion into just a hand signal. My hand signal is a flat hand moving in a "J" path. You can then gradually eliminate the hand signal.

COME

Reward value: Best

Difficulty: Easy

Need to know: Sit

Make sure you: Begin in a small room with no distractions.

---

1 Sitting on the floor with Fido, have a treat in your hand and allow Fido to wander. After a few seconds, call him — "Puppy puppy puppy!" in a happy, upbeat voice. When he comes to you, immediately treat and praise. Then ignore him and let him wander off to "reset" the exercise. *About 20 repetitions.*

After a few seconds, call Fido

When he reaches you, immediately treat and praise

2 Repeat Step 1, but stand up and call using his name. Say "Fido, Fido, Fido!" *About 10 repetitions.*

Stand up and call using his name   *Treat and praise when he reaches you*

3 Practice Step 2 in different rooms of the house, making sure that he comes in all situations. *About 20 repetitions.*

4 Call Fido (Step 2), but ask Fido for a sit when he reaches you. **M/R** when he sits. *About 10 repetitions.*

Ask for a sit when he reaches you   *M/R when he sits*

5 Change the command to "Fido, come!" (Still say it in a happy, upbeat voice.) When he comes, ask for a sit, then **M/R**. *About 10 repetitions.*

83

6 Repeat Step 5, but wait for him to sit voluntarily — don't give the command to sit. *About 20 repetitions.*

7 Practice outside. Allow Fido to wander, and when he looks a little bored with the yard, say, "Fido, Come!" When he comes, treat and praise him. Make it exciting! Continue practicing in gradually more distracting environments.

Note: *If during any of the above steps Fido isn't responding, move back to the previous step until he is succeeding, then move forward again. Always be sure to treat and praise Fido each time he comes to you; someday, his ability to respond could save his life.*

DOWN

Reward value: Better

Difficulty: Medium

Need to know: Sit

Note: *If Fido is having a difficult time, reward more often and for smaller accomplishments.*

I use one of two approaches for the Down command, depending on the pup. Different pups seem to do better with one or the other. Try both to determine which is most effective for your puppy.

Method 1

❶ Put Fido in a sit and let him nibble on a treat held between your forefinger and thumb until he is interested in it. Slowly move the treat straight down to the ground along the front of his chest; it should end up being on the ground between his two front paws, and he should be a little hunched over as he nibbles the treat. **M/R.** *About 3 repetitions.*

Put Fido in a sit and let him nibble a treat

Slowly move the treat straight down to the ground

The treat should end up being on the ground between his front paws, M/R.

❷ Repeat Step 1, but don't **M/R.** Move the treat along the floor slowly, away from him as he nibbles. The treat should make a path that is L-shaped (down along his chest, then out along the floor). As he follows the treat, he should stretch out into a down. **M/R.** *About 10 repetitions.*

Slowly move the treat along the floor away from Fido

As he follows, he should stretch into a down

When he lies down completely, M/R

85

❸ Repeat Step 3, but say the command "Down" as you lure Fido into the position. *About 15 repetitions.*

❹ Give the command "Down" as you make the same hand motion, but without a treat in your hand.

Method 2

❶ Put Fido in a sit and let him nibble on a treat held between your forefinger and thumb until he is interested in the treat. Move the treat slowly towards his rib cage as he continues to nibble. Then move it slowly towards the ground. Fido should fall into the down position. **M/R**. *About 10 repetitions.*

Put Fido in a sit and let him nibble a treat between your fingers

Move treat slowly towards his rib cage

Slowly move the treat towards the ground.

Fido should fall into the down position

M/R when he is fully down

❷ Repeat Step 1, but say the command "Down" as you lure Fido into the position. *About 15 repetitions.*

❸ Give the command "Down" as you make the same hand motion, but without a treat in your hand.

Note: *If he gets up at any point, start over and put him in the sit again. Never push him into the position. Let him end up in position on his own.*

You can gradually change your hand signal by making it less exact and more broad once Fido understands the command.

STAND

Reward value: Better

Difficulty: Easy

Need to know: Sit

---

❶ Begin with Fido in a sit position. Let Fido nibble on a treat in your hand, then move the treat straight away from him, approximately one foot. When Fido stands to get the treat, **M/R**. *About 5 repetitions.*

Begin with Fido in a sit and let him nibble a treat   *Move the treat away from him*   *M/R when Fido stands up*

87

❷ Begin with Fido in a sit. Let Fido nibble on a treat, then put the treat in your fist so Fido cannot see it. Move your fist away from Fido and say the cue for stand. When he stands up, **M/R**. *About 10 repetitions.*

❸ Begin with Fido in a sit. Put out your fist without a treat in it approximately one foot in front of Fido and say the cue for stand. When Fido stands up, **M/R**. *About 10 repetitions.*

HEEL

Reward value: Best

Difficulty: Hard

Need to know: Sit

Make sure you: Have a leash, and exercise Fido before beginning so he won't be too energetic to focus.

---

❶ Have Fido sit at your left side. Bend down and let him nibble on a treat in your left hand, but do not give it to him. Take one baby step forward with him still nibbling. When he stands up and takes a step forward to continue nibbling, **M/R**.
About 2 repetitions.

Have Fido sit at your left side

Let him nibble a treat in your left hand

Take one baby step forward. When he takes a step, M/R

2 Have Fido sit at your left side. Let him nibble on a treat. Take one baby step forward, and when he follows, lure him into a sit with the treat. **M/R**. *About 2 repetitions.*

Have Fido sit at your left side and let him nibble a treat

Take one baby step forward

When he follows, lure him into a sit

When he sits, M/R

89

③ Repeat Step 3, but take two steps forward. *About 2 repetitions.*

④ Gradually increase the steps you take before rewarding until you can take 10 steps with Fido walking beside you, nibbling the treat. *Repeat each amount of steps 2 times.*

⑤ Hold the treat a bit higher where he is reaching up (but not jumping) to nibble; his nose should be pointed to the ceiling. Begin again with one step, the sit, **M/R**. Gradually increase the steps taken until you can walk 10 steps with Fido beside you, looking up at you the majority of the time. *About 2 repetitions.*

Hold the treat a bit higher   *Take one step*   *Stop and have him sit.*
Then M/R.

⑥ Repeat Step 5, but hold the treat in your left fist at your stomach and gradually increase the steps taken.

90

STEP # 6 - Hold the treat in your left fist at your stomach

7 Put the leash on Fido and hold it loosely in your right hand so there is no tension and Fido doesn't realize it is on. Give "heel" command and walk a few steps, stop and **M/R** after he sits. If he gets confused, lure him with a treat once or twice and try again.

8 Gradually increase the distractions. If he ever leaves heel position, give a gentle and short tug on the leash to remind him to stay beside you.

With this method, Fido never views the leash as confining, and there is no fighting the leash. The dog learns to walk nicely beside you.

Step #7

The one difficulty with this is that until you have him walking politely beside you, you can't take him on a walk to get his exercise out. This means that you must find another method for the first week or two. Some suggestions can be found in Chapter 4 under "Exercise."

If it is absolutely necessary for you to walk your puppy to get the energy out before you can teach him to heel fully, then you will need to leash-train him.

LEASH TRAINING

Put the leash on the puppy with a buckle or martingale, see pages 162-163. Walk forward and encourage the puppy and talk to him. At first, he will probably follow you, but eventually the pup will feel the tension on the leash and brace himself against it.

When this happens, stop walking but continue to pull the leash. Use enough pressure to make it uncomfortable, but don't use so much that the puppy is being moved by the leash. After a few seconds of the tension, most puppies will give in and hop up towards the pressure — immediately praise the puppy! (Don't give him a treat for this because some pups will learn to brace themselves just so they get a treat when they give in).

After a few days of this, the pup will learn to give in to the pressure of the leash quickly so it goes away, and he will walk nicely beside you.

If Fido pulls ahead of you, immediately stop walking and keep your arm and the leash still. When Fido stops pulling, calmly ask him to return to your heel at your left side - either by luring him with your hand or using gentle pressure of the leash. Then when he returns to the correct position mark it, and begin walking forward. Repeat each time he pulls ahead.

The goal is to have a "J" of slack in the leash. Even if it's necessary to leash-train Fido first, I always recommend to continue to train "heel" because it teaches the pup to be focused on you and obeying, rather than being controlled by the leash.

SIT-STAY

Reward value: Better

Difficulty: Medium

Need to know: Sit

Make sure you: Train in an area without distractions.

Always begin with Fido in a sit position at your left side, facing forward.

❶ Give the command "Stay" with the hand signal, then take a baby step forward and pivot so you are in front of Fido, facing him. Immediately pivot back and **M/R**. *About 5 repetitions.*

Give the command "Stay" with the hand signal

Take a baby step forward and pivot so you are in front of Fido

Immediately pivot back and M/R

❷ Give your command/hand signal, then pivot in front and take one step backwards. Then immediately return and pivot to your original position. **M/R**. *About 3 repetitions.*

93

③ Repeat Step 2, but take two steps back. *About 3 repetitions.*

④ Repeat Step 2, but take three steps back. *About 3 repetitions.*

⑤ Continually add one step until Fido stays when you take at least 10 steps back and return, repeating each increase three times.

⑥ Give the stay command/hand signal, then walk two steps straight away from your dog (don't pivot). Then turn around and walk back to original position. **M/R**. *About 5 repetitions.*

⑦ Repeat Step 6, but take three steps away. *About 5 repetitions.*

⑧ Repeat Step 6, but take four steps. *About 5 repetitions.*

⑨ Continually add one step until Fido stays when you walk straight away from him for 10 steps and return. *Repeat each increase 5 times.*

⑩ Give the command to stay, walk 10 steps away, turn around to face him, wait two seconds, then walk back and **M/R**. *About 5 repetitions.*

⑪ Repeat Step 10, but wait three seconds. *About 5 repetitions.*

⑫ Add one second more at a time to gradually increase how long Fido must stay. Repeat each additional second 5 times.

Note: *If you wish to train Fido to stay longer than 15 seconds, continue training by gradually adding time; usually you will be able to add three or five seconds more at a time once he can stay for 15 seconds.*

If you wish to teach Fido to stay when you go farther away than 10 steps, continue training by taking one additional step, then returning and rewarding.

Don't increase time and distance at the same time; increase one at a time so Fido doesn't get overwhelmed. If he lies down or stands up during any of the steps, guide him back to the starting point, ask for a sit, and start over. If he leaves postion three times in a row, go back to the previous step so he has a solid understanding of what's expected.

DOWN-STAY

Reward value: Better

Difficulty: Medium

Need to know: Down

Make sure you: Train in an area without distractions.

---

❶ Repeat the "Sit Stay" steps, but begin with Fido in Down.

> **Note:** *If he gets out of position, just take his collar, guide him back to his starting position, ask for a down, and start over.*

As always, if he leaves position three times in a row, go back to the previous step so he has a solid understanding of what's expected.

Chapter 7

- Leave it
- Drop
- Touch
- Place
- Finish
- Recall

Additional Lessons

LEAVE IT

Reward value: Good and Best

Difficulty: Easy

❶ Sit on the ground with Fido in front of you. Put a low-value treat on the ground and a high-value treat in your non-dominant hand or somewhere easily accessible — but don't draw Fido's attention to it.

Put a low-value treat on the ground

❷ As soon as Fido attempts to get the low-value treat, cover it with your dominant hand. (Be quick!) Fido may lick or paw your hand in an attempt to get the treat, but ignore it.

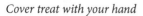

Cover treat with your hand

③ Keep your hand over the treat until Fido voluntarily looks up at your face, then **M/R** with the high-value treat in your hand. Immediately pick up the low-value reward from the floor.

Keep hand over treat until Fido looks at your face

M/R with the high-value treat in your hand

④ Repeat Steps 1-3 about 10 times. Fido should begin to ignore the treat on the floor and instead look up at your face, so you will not need to cover the treat. The first few times Fido does this, **M/R** with lots of praise!

⑤ Add in the command "Leave it," then repeat Steps 1-3. *About 10 repetitions.*

⑥ Gradually increase the amount of time that Fido must leave the treat on the ground.

DROP

Reward value: Best

Difficulty: Easy

Make sure you: Have a Low to Medium valued toy

---

❶ Get Fido interested in the toy by wiggling it on the ground until he begins to tug on it.

❷ Allow Fido to play for three seconds or so with you and the toy. Gently pull on the toy and move it from side to side slowly to interact with him.

98

❸ Stop moving the toy (have your hand go limp but keep hold of the toy), and say "Drop."

Stop moving the toy   *Say "Drop"*

❹ When he lets go of the toy, immediately give him a high-value treat and praise. Then, give him the tug command and begin playing again. *Repeat.*

When he lets go of the toy   ***M/R***

Note: *If he doesn't let go of the toy voluntarily within five seconds, repeat the command and at the same time present the treat — he will drop the toy to eat. After two or three repetitions, just say "drop" and wait for him to release the toy. Transition quickly from needing to present the treat to just saying drop, so he doesn't learn to only drop the toy when you show him the treat — that's just bribery.*

Never take away something your dog values without giving him something in return. Otherwise, he may begin to protect his food or toys by snapping at you because you are a threat.

TOUCH

Reward value: Better

Difficulty: Easy

Note: *The Touch command is useful for positioning Fido or to get him to stand.*

❶ Have Fido in front of you and treats nearby, easily accessible. Present your hand out flat in front of Fido's nose, about three inches away. Fido will lean forward to sniff your hand. **M/R**. *About 5 repetitions.*

Present your hand in front of Fido   *Fido will lean forward to sniff it*   *When he sniffs it, M/R*

❷ Raise the criteria — only **M/R** when Fido makes contact with your hand. As soon as his nose touches your hand, **M/R**. *About 15 repetitions.*

❸ Only **M/R** when Fido puts a little more pressure on your hand, showing confidence. *About 15 repetitions.*

❹ Add the cue you want him to learn, present your hand and **M/R** when he touches it.

Note: *I often see Fido thinking about touching my hand and I anticipate it, marking too early. Sometimes I must close my eyes to accurately **M/R**.*

PLACE

Reward value: Better

Difficulty: Medium

Make sure to: Use a blanket or bed as Fido's "place."

Note: *The Place command is useful for dinnertime or when company is visiting.*

Begin with Fido beside you and the object called "place" flat on the ground.

❶ When your dog shows any interest whatsoever (looks at it, sniffs it, etc.), **M/R**. *About 5 repetitions.*

Begin with place on the ground

Fido shows interest in the object

M/R

❷ **M/R** when your dog steps on it. *About 5 repetitions.*

❸ **M/R** when your dog puts two paws on the blanket/bed. *About 5 repetitions.*

❹ **M/R** when he puts three paws on the blanket/bed. *About 5 repetitions.*

⑤ **M/R** when all four paws are on the blanket/bed, then ask for a down, and **M/R** again. *About 10 repetitions.*

When all four paws are on blanket, ask for a down

When Fido goes down, M/R

⑥ When Fido starts going toward the blanket/bed, say his cue for "place." When he is fully on the blanket/bed and lays down, **M/R**. *About 10 repetitions.*

⑦ Say Fido's cue for "place," and when Fido goes onto the blanket/bed, and lays down, count to three, then **M/R**. Give his release word and encourage him off the blanket/bed. *About 10 repetitions.*

⑧ Say Fido's cue for "place," **M/R** when he lays down on the blanket/bed, then count to five and **M/R** again. Give the release word and encourage him off the blanket/bed. *About 10 repetitions.*

⑨ Continue to gradually increase the time spent on the blanket/bed. With continued practice, Fido can learn to stay there, until released even for an hour or more.

102

FINISH

Reward value: Better

Difficulty: Medium

Need to know: Come; Sit

Note: *This is a command used in obedience competitions; the purpose is to have the dog move from sitting in front of you into heel position (sitting at your left side).*

Begin standing up with Fido sitting, facing you.

1 Let Fido nibble on a treat, then slowly lure him to your right side and behind you. *About 5 repetitions.*

Begin with Fido sitting, facing you

Lure Fido to your right side

Continue luring him behind you, then M/R

2 Repeat Step 1, but continue luring him so he walks behind you and ends on your left side. *About 5 repetitions.*

Continue luring him behind you

Continue luring until he is on your left side

3 Repeat Step 2, but ask for a sit when he is at your left side, parallel to you. **M/R.** *About 10 repetitions.*

Ask for a sit when he reaches your left side.

When he sits, M/R

4 Repeat Step 3, but give the command for "Finish" as you are luring him. *About 10 repetitions.*

RECALL

Reward value: Better

Difficulty: Hard

Need to know: Sit Stay, Come, Finish

Note: *This is used in many obedience competitions. Only practice this with Fido if he has mastered the commands needed, as you want to set him up for success rather than failure.*

1. Begin with Fido in heel position (in a sit at your left side, parallel to you).

2. Give the command for "Stay."

3. Walk about 20 feet straight away from Fido, then turn to face him.

4. Give Fido's command for "Come."

5. After he sits in front of you, give the command for "Finish."

6. When Fido completes the "Finish" and is sitting at your left side, **M/R**.

Chapter 8

IN THIS CHAPTER

- High five
- Spin
- Roll over
- Paws up
- Sit pretty

Tricks

Tricks

STEP #1
Hold treat on palm, with thumb, in front of Fido

STEP #1
M/R

STEP #1
Fido tries to use his paw.

HIGH FIVE

Reward value: Best

Difficulty: Easy

1. Show Fido a treat, then hold it against your palm with your thumb. Present your hand in front of Fido as if you are expecting a high-five. Let Fido nibble and try to get the treat. When he tries to use his paw, **M/R** with the treat. *About 10 repetitions, five in each hand.*

2. Present your hand in the same way as Step 1, but do not have a treat in the hand. When Fido paws your hand, **M/R**. *About 10 repetitions, five in each hand.*

3. Say the cue for "High-five," then present your hand. When Fido paws it, **M/R**.

   Note: *If in the first few steps he won't use his paw, then move your hand closer to his paw on the ground. As soon as he picks up his paw a tiny bit, **M/R**. Gradually raise the criteria, and only **M/R** when he picks up his paw a little further, then only **M/R** when he moves his paw towards you, etc.*

SPIN

Reward value: Better

Difficulty: Easy

STEP #1 - Slowly move your hand in a circle so he follows and goes in a circle himself. M/R

❶ Let Fido nibble on a treat between your finger and thumb, then bend over and move your hand slowly in a circle so he follows it and goes in a circle himself. **M/R**. *About 20 repetitions, 10 in each direction.*

❷ Repeat Step 1, but without a treat in your hand and say the command for "Spin." Replicate the hand motion so Fido thinks you have a treat. **M/R**. *About 10 repetitions.*

3 Bring your hand further up, so Fido isn't following your hand directly, but still make a large circular motion with your hand. **M/R**. Next time, make a little smaller circular motion with your hand. Gradually change your hand signal until you can spin your finger in a small circle, and he will spin.

ROLL OVER

Reward value: Best

Difficulty: Medium

Need to know: Down

STEP #1 - Slowly move the treat towards his side

1 Begin with Fido in a down position and let him nibble on a treat. Slowly move the treat towards his side. If he follows the treat, until your hand is touching his side, **M/R**.

Continue moving treat to his opposite side

When he rolls over completely, M/R

109

2 Repeat Step 1, but without rewarding, continue moving the treat to the opposite side of him so he is lying on his back, then rolls all the way over, **M/R**.
About 10 repetitions.

3 Say the cue for "Roll over" and repeat Step 2. *About 10 repetitions.*

4 Lure Fido into rolling over, but without a treat in your hand. Repeat your normal hand motion, and have a treat nearby to reward him. **M/R** when he rolls over.
About 20 repetitions.

5 Gradually, you can make your hand signal less obvious so you have a simple hand signal. *Repeat each version of your hand signal. About 5 repetitions.*

PAWS UP

Reward value: Better

Difficulty: Medium

Make Sure: Have an object for Fido to put his paws up on, elbow height or lower.

Method 1

❶ Encourage Fido up on the object by patting it. If Fido gets up, **M/R**. *About 10 repetitions.*

❷ Say the cue for "Paws up," then encourage him up. **M/R**. *About 20 repetitions.*

Method 2

Gradually move the treat toward the object

Keep moving it until Fido walks into object and lifts foot to step over it

Continue moving the treat so he puts both paws on object, M/R

❶ Put the object in front of Fido. Let Fido nibble on a treat and gradually move the treat to the object. Keep moving it until Fido walks into the object and lifts his foot to step over it. **M/R**. *About 5 repetitions.*

❷ Lure Fido so he puts one paw on the object, then continue slowly moving the treat so he puts both front paws on it. **M/R**. *About 10 repetitions.*

❸ Without a treat in your hand, lure Fido so both paws are on the object and say the cue for "Paws up." **M/R**. *About 5 repetitions.*

111

④ Gently pat the object, encouraging Fido to get his front two paws on the object, and say the command for "Paws up." As soon as both paws are on the object, **M/R**. *About 10 repetitions.*

⑤ Point to the object, give the cue for "Paws up" and **M/R** when Fido gets up.

SIT PRETTY

Reward value: Best

Difficulty: Hard

Need to know: Sit

Note: *This takes a lot of abdominal muscles so it can take a dog from one week to three months to learn, depending on the age and build of your dog. Don't rush because it might be uncomfortable or impossible for your pup to do.*

❶ Put Fido in a sit and let him nibble on a treat. Then slowly move the treat up above his head, making sure he is still nibbling it. As soon as Fido's front paws come off the ground, **M/R**. *About five repetitions.*

Put Fido in a sit and let him nibble a treat

Slowly move treat above his head

When his front paws come off ground, M/R

② Lure Fido into sitting upright (Step 1), but continue holding the treat above him for longer amounts of time, working up to about five seconds. *About 3 repetitions per added second.*

③ Say the cue for "Sit pretty," then lure him into position. **M/R** after five seconds of sitting up. *About 10 repetitions.*

④ Lure him into the position without a treat. As soon as he sits up, **M/R**.

⑤ Lure him into the position without a treat and **M/R** after two seconds. Then increase the time he sits up until he reaches five seconds. *About 3 repetitions per added second.*

113

Chapter 9

- **Games**
  Hide and seek
  Pushups
  Tug o' war

- **Activities to do with your dog**

Fun with Fido

Games

HIDE AND SEEK

Reward value: Good

Difficulty: Easy

Need to know: Come

❶ One person holds Fido's collar. Another goes to an adjacent room and stands out of sight.

❷ The person hiding calls Fido in a happy, upbeat voice. As soon as that person calls, the holder releases Fido's collar.

❸ As Fido searches, the person hiding praises him.

❹ The hider **M/R** when Fido finds him or her. Make it very exciting with lots of praise; they can even play a short game of tug, or throw a toy for him in addition to the treat.

5 After a few repetitions, the hider and the person holding Fido can switch so he learns to come to anyone who calls him. The hiding places can become increasingly more difficult. Begin simply with going to another room, then move to a closet, then under the bed, etc.

PUSH-UPS

Reward value: Better

Difficulty: Easy

Need to know: Sit; Down

Note: *A push-up is when Fido goes from a sit into a down or a down into a sit. It's a great way to practice basic obedience with your pup.*

1 With a treat ready, tell Fido to "Sit." **M/R** when he obeys.

2 Give the command for "Down." **M/R** when he lies down.

3 Give the command for "Sit." **M/R** when he sits.

4 Give the command for "Down." **M/R** when he lies down.

Sit

Down

Sit

Down

Note: *Going from a down to a sit is often more difficult for Fido. If he doesn't understand, then lure him with the treat into the sit, and* **M/R**. *Use the lure three times, then repeat the hand motion the fourth time as if you had the lure, but you don't have a treat in your hand.* **M/R** *when he follows your hand and sits. It's good to play tug or fetch in between so Fido doesn't get bored.*

FETCH

Reward value: Better

Difficulty: Medium to hard, depending on the dog

Need to know: Drop and Tug

Make sure you: Use a small toy that is easy for Fido to grasp

117

Method 1

Toss the toy a few feet away from Fido.

1 When he picks it up, praise him softly and encourage him to bring it back to you by patting your leg or the floor.

2 When Fido brings it back, play a game of tug or give him a better-value treat.

3 Repeat Steps 1 and 2. *About 15 repetitions.*

4 When Fido is bringing the toy back to you quickly, throw the toy farther and farther away.

Note: *If he drops it after picking it up, try again. Keep it upbeat and fun no matter how Fido does.*

Method 2

1 Begin playing tug with Fido.

2 When Fido is playing the game excitedly, let go of the toy.

3 Pat your leg and encourage him to come to you with the toy in his mouth.

4 When he gets to you, praise him and begin playing tug again.

5 After a few seconds of tug, ask for a "Drop." (Page 98)

6 Repeat Steps 1 to 5. *About 20 repetitions.*

7 Without playing tug first, gently toss the toy a few feet away from you and Fido.

8 When Fido picks it up, encourage him to bring it to you, just as before.

9 Praise when he gets to you and begin an exciting game of tug.

10 Repeat Steps 7 to 9. *About 10 repetitions.*

TUG O' WAR

Playing tug o' war with dogs is a debated topic in the dog training field. In my opinion, tug is a great game as long as there are clear rules and boundaries. It can improve your relationship with your dog because it is so enjoyable for Fido.

Rules for Fido

- Fido must obey the "Drop" command at any point in the game when you ask.

- Fido's teeth must never ever touch skin.

TEACHING FIDO TO NOT TOUCH YOUR SKIN

1. Play tug with your puppy for a few days so he understands the game.

2. After a few play sessions, get the tug toy out and grasp it with both hands like you are trying to stretch the toy, leaving just enough space between your hands for the dog's mouth to fit in. Initiate tugging.

3. If Fido touches you with his teeth at all, say "Ouch!" and take the toy away for five seconds.

4. Repeat Steps 2 and 3 two more times.

5. After the third time he touches your hand while tugging and you yelp "Ouch," the game is over. Put the toy away and don't play for another few hours.

- Fido must only tug on command. Having a command will keep him from trying to tug with household items during times other than play sessions. If he thinks every time you move something he should tug, you will get very frustrated.

- Fido cannot become possessive. Play growling is fine, but some dogs can't play tug with people because they begin guarding the toy. Most dogs don't do this, especially if you are frequently asking for a "Drop." If Fido shows any signs of guarding, immediately stop the game and walk away. Don't worry about getting Fido to drop, because he might be dangerous at this point.

Signs of guarding

- Staring harshly at you without blinking

- Hackles raised

- Snarling, lips curled, showing teeth

- Snapping

Rules for you

- Only match the intensity of your dog. Never go above it, or he might get frightened and not play.

- Be gentle enough to not hurt his teeth.

- Never dangle the toy above Fido's head. This is a fantastic way to accidentally get your hand bitten, and teach your dog to jump on people.

- Ask for a "Drop" every 10 to 15 seconds. This keeps the game under control. If Fido releases as soon as you ask, then give the tug command and continue playing. If he doesn't, ask one more time; if he still won't let go, take the toy from him and end the game. Then practice the command "Drop" before playing tug again.

What toys should be used for playing tug o' war?

I prefer toys that are long, around one to two feet, so Fido has plenty of room to avoid my hands and not cause the game to end. Long, braided fleece toys are perfect for this. They come in many colors and lengths. You can even make them yourself.

121

Activities to do with your dog

4-H Dog Club

4-H dog clubs are for youth ages 8 to 19. In most clubs, youth learn about dog care, training and showing, as well as developing good responsibility. I recommend all youth get involved in a 4-H dog club if possible.

Agility

Agility is an obstacle course for dogs that handlers direct them through. The purpose of agility is to demonstrate the handler's and dog's teamwork, focus, concentration and athletic ability. It is a timed event, but a high score is more important than a speedy run; a single dropped bar will disqualify the team. Agility classes are a great way to bond with your dog while being focused and keeping a healthy, respectful relationship.

Disc dog (Frisbee dogs)

Disc dog competitions have a few variations. One variation is the "Toss and Fetch," in which the team is awarded points for the distances at which the disc is caught by the dog in 60 seconds — extra points are awarded for catches made in mid-air. Another variation is a freestyle event. In the freestyle event the team has a choreographed routine prepared that includes music and multiple discs. Judges give the team a score for their performance in multiple categories such as degree of difficulty, canine athleticism, and showmanship.

Flyball

Flyball is a relay race consisting of four dogs per team. Teams race at the same time, with dogs running the 51-foot lane and jumping over four hurdles to reach the spring-loaded box that shoots out a tennis ball.

When the dog hits the box, he must catch the ball and race back across the lane and four hurdles, carrying the tennis ball across the finish line. As soon as one dog finishes, the next dog must be released to run the course. If any mistake is made, that dog must re-run the course after the other dogs have completed their turns.

This is a very fast-paced competition, and electronic sensors are used, as many of the races are extremely close.

Conformation

This is the typical "dog show." The handlers stack the dogs and parade around the ring with them as the judge observes each dog's form and movement. Judges evaluate the appearance and structure of each dog because the purpose of Conformation is to determine which dogs will produce the best puppies to maintain and improve breed standards. As a result, only purebred, registered dogs are permitted to compete.

Dock diving

Dock diving is a quickly growing sport. A toy is thrown into a pool and the dog is released to jump as far as he can.

The distance the dog jumps is measured from the point where the base of his tail hit the water. This is a great sport for water dogs, such as Labrador Retrievers.

124

Obedience

AKC® obedience competitions feature the dogs that have been trained to behave in all circumstances and with many distractions.

There are multiple levels of obedience classes, beginning with only on-lead exercises up to completely off-lead exercises without verbal commands, and including scent discrimination exercises.

Herding

Herding trials are competitions in which dogs must move sheep across fields, through gates, into rings, etc. (Like the movie *Babe*.) Usually only dogs from the herding category participate in these trials, and the most popular dog seen is the Border Collie.

Each team begins with a maximum score, and the judges deduct points for each fault. There is a time limit, but there is not an advantage to completing the course in the least amount of time.

9

Tracking

Tracking competitions demonstrate a dog's ability to detect a scent and follow it, which is the foundation of search-and-rescue work.

This activity is completely up to the dog, as the handler does not know the correct route and has no way to judge whether his or her dog is following the correct scent. The handler can only trust the dog and follow behind.

This is a great activity for those dog owners who love spending time outside as well as working with their dogs.

Rally

AKC Rally® is similar to the obedience competitions, but a little more laid-back, and with handlers following instructions on signs rather than those given from a judge.

This is a timed event, but the time is only considered when two competitors have the same score for accuracy.

Unlike in Obedience, Rally handlers are allowed and encouraged to talk to their dogs and give multiple commands. Rally encourages handlers and their dogs to have fun while competing and promotes a good relationship.

9

127

Chapter 10

- Puppy development
- Choosing your puppy

What age?

Shelter or breeder?

Male or female?

- Dog groups and purposes
- Jobs for dogs

From Puppy to Dog

Puppy development

Early Critical Period — Birth to 3 weeks

Neonatal (Birth to 12 days): When puppies are born, their world is very limited. Blind, with a minimal sense of smell and no useful hearing, they seek comfort. The puppy's brainwaves are the same sleeping as awake, so there is not much mental activity. At 10 to 14 days old, the eyes and ears begin to open.

Transitional (13 to 20 days): Many physical changes happen! The eyes open at day 13, ear canals open, teeth begin to erupt (causing them to begin biting/chewing), the tail be-

gins to wag, and there is communal vocalization. At 3 weeks old, there are significant changes in brainwaves. Also at 3 weeks, the pups should begin to have careful interaction with humans.

Socialization Period — 3 to 12 weeks

3 to 7 weeks — Canine socialization: At about weeks three and four, the pups begin attempting to walk. Pups need to learn about their species. They learn to play, to bite, the body language to use, etc. They also learn about discipline. The mother weans them through discipline, and other pups teach them that playing ends when they bite too hard. If pups can't complete this stage with their littermates, then the dogs may become noisy, aggressive and harder to control as adults.

7 to 12 weeks — Human socialization: Pups are dependent on their mother until they are weaned at about seven to eight weeks old. When you get your puppy — usually at eight weeks — he will most likely be taken from his siblings for the first time, so he will need to be handled and comforted often. Puppies will follow humans around at first because the wide-open world is scary, but he will become less scared and more curious as he gets older. This is why it's important to start training from the very beginning — so you can keep your puppy safe when he starts to mature and you can teach him from the first day which behaviors are acceptable and which are not.

This is also the best time for the pup to go to a new home. Fido needs to be separated from his mom and littermates to build self-confidence. The bonding peak is between six and eight weeks, so this is the prime time to introduce a new human — you! At 49 days, the brainwaves are the same as an adult dog, so training should begin immediately. New experiences and socialization are crucial during the puppy's life from seven to twelve weeks. Often many dog owners wait until their puppy receives all his shots before socializing him. The issue with this is that puppies don't get all their shots until they are five to six months old, and at this point they have already passed the socialization period. The chances of your puppy getting one of the diseases is minimal; the chance that your dog will be nervous in new situations and aggressive if you don't socialize him is much greater. I take the minor risk and socialize my pups. Stay away from pet stores and dog parks because so many dogs visit those places, often without any shots or vet history. Other than that, the pups go to all sorts of areas, stores that allow dogs (home improvement stores often do), regular parks, or soccer games, etc.

Seniority classification period — 12 to 16 weeks: The pups begin to test the hierarchy and determine which pups are in charge of the others. Studies have shown that if two pups are kept from the same litter in one family until this age, only one of the puppies is capable of becoming a guide dog. In other words, only one was able to reach his maximum potential. It is never recommended to raise littermates to adulthood together because it affects their success.

Adolescence

Around 4 months old, your puppy starts to become an adolescent. He begins to grow up and is a "teenager." Physically, your dog will be going through an awkward phase, as his legs seem too long for his body, and he might seem skinny.

It's very important that his training continues through this stage, because many times adolescent dogs will test the boundaries and rules of the household. He should also continue to be socialized.

CHALLENGES OF ADOLESCENCE

Unlearning: Occasionally, an adolescent dog will seem to not know the commands and behaviors he previously did. It can be frustrating because Fido looks like an adult dog, but is acting like an 8-week-old puppy. Be patient and reteach the commands. Soon your dog will grow up and everything will come back to him — just be sure not to lose your patience, as it is an important time to continue building up trust.

Selective deafness: Fido may decide the leaves on the ground are more interesting than you calling him, so he will just not respond. Often Fido starts tuning you out, or at least pretending to, and won't respond if he feels he doesn't need to. Sometimes you need to up the ante and use higher-value treats to make it worth his while until he gets out of this stage.

Teenager behavior: Prepare for overall exuberance. Breeds such as Labrador Retrievers, Golden Retrievers and Brittany Spaniels can be extremely energetic during this stage. They will seem to be bouncing off the walls, always in the way and clumsy. As a result, teenage Fido will need more exercise to try to minimize this. This is a great time to get into dog sports such as agility, flyball, Frisbee, etc. since Fido has all this energy and you might be bored with the usual obedience exercises.

132

Increase in aggression: Some dogs, especially protective breeds, will have a sudden increase in territorial protection and overall aggression. This needs to be watched carefully, and the correct action should be taken. If your goal was to have a dog that will warn you of strangers approaching, then barking at strangers should be allowed. If this was not the goal, then redirect his attention to something appropriate when he does this.

Fear of new situations: At some point between 6 and 14 months, puppies often go through another fear period that lasts approximately two weeks, very similar to the first one. Traumatic experiences should be avoided, and new experiences should be positive and enjoyable. When your puppy becomes scared of something that is not worthy of fear (such as a bush or a statue in the yard), perform a "Jolly routine" — going up to the "scary" object, laughing and having a conversation with it. Don't force Fido to come any closer to the object than he feels comfortable. As you laugh and talk to the scary object, Fido will become curious and start to investigate since you have indicated you don't see it as a threat.

Adulthood

Most dogs have reached their full size at 18 months, but large breeds sometimes take a few more months. Dogs are not fully mature mentally until they are about three years old. However, dogs older than three can learn just as many tricks and behaviors. The phrase "You can't teach an old dog new tricks" is not true! Older dogs love being trained, too.

Choosing your puppy

What age?

Your chances of having a successful relationship with your dog are exponentially better if you begin with a puppy. I suggest getting one that is 8 to 10 weeks old from a shelter or quality breeder.

I do not usually recommend first time dog owners adopt an older dog unless they have had the opportunity to perform multiple behavioral tests on him, preferably with a trainer along.

While I believe that all shelter dogs should have homes, there are many unknowns when adopting an older dog. You do not know the dog's past and what quirks, fears, or habits he or she might have acquired. Because of this, adopting an adult dog is a gamble. There have been many wonderful stories and great experiences from people bringing an adult shelter dog into their homes, but not all stories are successful.

Shelter or breeder?

Shelter puppy

Pros

- Saving a life
- Low adoption fee
- Keeps strays off the streets
- Immediately available

Cons

- No background history
- Uncertainty of the breed (temperament, size, etc.)
- Possibility of genetic medical complications

Responsible breeder

Pros

- Health testing and guarantees
- Breed certainty
- Return policy — Breeders often know the pups' temperament and can recommend a certain pup based on what the buyer is looking for.
- Parents (or at least the dam) are usually available to visit so that potential owners see the predicted temperament, size and appearance of the pups.

Cons

- Cost
- Takes time; often the pups aren't available immediately and you must wait until they are old enough to leave the litter.

135

Male or Female?

For most breeds, there is not much difference in temperament or looks between the genders when they are spayed/neutered. (I always suggest spaying or neutering your dog, as it makes life a lot less complicated and frustrating.)

On the whole, though, females tend to be more moody and have the mentality of "things will be done on my terms." Males can be more pushy and demanding for things like affection, food, etc., but are usually more stable and laid back.

If you know the breed your pup will be, research to determine whether there is a large difference in the male and female temperament. Choose based on what characteristics you would like Fido to have. An example of a breed in which gender matters is Border Collies. Male Border Collies tend to be more laid-back (well, for a Border Collie at least), while the females are more driven and some say they don't have an "off switch." Females are always "on the job," whether it's herding sheep or moving all the shoes into a pile in the living room.

Dog groups and purposes

Each breed of dog was created for a purpose. Knowing this purpose is essential in picking a puppy. If you know the purpose, then you know what to expect from your adult dog and whether that fits your lifestyle.

Below are the seven American Kennel Club (AKC®) categories of breeds with a general description and examples. (Before bringing a dog into your home, research the breed more thoroughly to find out if the dog's traits match up with the breed category traits.)

HERDING GROUP

Herding dogs are unique. They have the ability to control groups of other animals. Most are highly driven and have exceptional instincts. They were bred to herd animals — anything from chickens to cattle to horses. These dogs have been very useful in the history of man, and are still used in ranches now.

Temperament: Loyal, driven, energetic, intelligent

Tendencies: Nipping at heels, chasing animals or moving objects

Examples: Border Collie, Shetland Sheepdog, Pembroke Welsh Corgi, Belgian Malinois

10

137

HOUND GROUP

Hounds were bred primarily for their exceptional hunting ability. Many of the dogs in this group have exceptional scenting ability. Some are called "sight hounds," meaning they have been bred to chase an animal they can see, and to have stamina as they sprint toward the prey.

Temperament: Laid back, loyal

Tendencies: Following a scent, chasing prey, howling, barking

Examples: Bloodhound, Beagle, Afghan Hound, Dachshund

TERRIER GROUP

Terriers were bred to hunt mice and other vermin. Small pests hide in the ground, and the dogs are expected to smell them and dig after them. When they are caught, the dogs

are to "dispose" of them — kill them. This has a huge effect on the characteristics of dogs in this category.

Temperament: Energetic, intelligent, opinionated

Tendencies: Digging, barking

Examples: Jack Russell terrier, Wheaton terrier, Airedale terrier

NONSPORTING GROUP

The nonsporting group is the most diverse, and the dogs actually have very little in common. This group is a little like a catchall group.

Examples: Dalmatian, French Bulldog, Finnish Spitz

SPORTING GROUP

Sporting breeds are usually good-natured and well-rounded dogs. They have various uses, but are known for their aptitude in water and wooded areas.

Temperament: Energetic, loyal, friendly

Tendencies: Swimming, retrieving

Examples: Golden Retriever, Brittany Spaniel, Irish Setter, Pointer

10

139

TOY GROUP

Toy breeds were bred mainly to provide companionship. They are popular in large cities because of their small size, but they are by no means fragile. This group's main commonality is their size.

Temperament: Alert, playful

Tendencies: Barking, cuddling

Examples: Cavalier King Charles Spaniel, Pug, Pomeranian

WORKING GROUP

The dogs in this group were bred for a wide variety of tasks — from guarding livestock to pulling sleds to hunting big game. They are all large, and most have a high exercise requirement. They need firm, consistent training and strong leadership.

Temperament: Protective, moderate to high energy

Tendencies: Pulling on a lead, stubbornness

Examples: Anatolian Shepherd, Greater Swiss Mountain Dog, Siberian Husky

Jobs for dogs

Service (or assistance) dogs

Dogs that are trained to mitigate their handler's disability are called service dogs or assistance dogs. These dogs go through months, often years, of specialized training. Because a service dog is a tool to aid a person with a disability, the dogs are granted public access, meaning they can go with their handler anywhere that the public is allowed to go. Although not required, service dogs often have vests or harnesses on, showing they are service dogs.

Guide dogs: Help direct people with impaired vision. The dogs lead the handler, avoiding objects and stopping at curbs, stairs, etc. to prevent the handler from tripping, falling or running into objects.

Medical alert/response dogs: Alert their handler to an impending medical issue or they help a person once the medical problem has begun. Types include diabetic alert dogs, seizure response dogs and allergen alert dogs, among others.

Hearing alert dogs: Alert their handlers to noises that they are not able to hear. For example, some people cannot hear sounds in a certain range, such as doorbells and fire alarms. The dogs alert the handler when the sounds occur, in order to keep him or her safe.

10

Mobility assistance dogs: Help people with a mobility-related disability. Some people have a disability that results in dizziness at times, or weakness. The dogs are trained to brace themselves and support the handler when needed. They also help the handler get up from a sitting position, or if the handler falls they are taught to stand still as the handler pushes on the dog to stand up. These dogs are chosen from large breeds so they can support the handler's weight.

Therapy dogs

Dogs are trained to provide affection and comfort to people in hospitals, retirement homes, nursing homes, schools, people with learning difficulties and those in stressful situations, such as disaster areas.

These dogs are often confused with service dogs, but they are very different. Therapy dogs are not granted public access and are not for a person with a disability. The handler visits places where people can benefit from the comfort or enjoyment of interacting with a dog. Therapy dogs need to be well trained, but there are no laws regarding them. The handler must get approval from the facility where they wish to bring the dog.

Emotional support dogs

Emotional support dogs give comfort to their handlers. These dogs are not granted public access, but they are allowed on planes or in pet-restricted housing as long as a doctor's note declaring the animal is helpful is presented.

Emotional support dogs help someone whose doctor considers the dog to be helpful for his or her health. Unlike service dogs and therapy dogs, emotional support dogs do not have to be trained at all.

142

Police dogs

Some police dogs are "detector dogs," meaning they alert to bombs, drugs, firearms or other dangerous substances. Their alerting behavior can be either aggressive or passive,

depending on what material they are trained to find. Dogs trained to find bombs, for example, are taught a passive alert — sitting or something else that doesn't require touching the object. Dogs trained to find drugs, however, might be taught an aggressive alert, such as to paw at the drugs, before being rewarded.

Other police dogs are trained to attack criminals when commanded. The dogs are faster and more agile than police officers, and are trained to run full speed at the specified person and target a certain area — such as the arm — to slow down or bring down the person. They are also taught to run toward the sound of gunfire; this puts the dog in the potential path of a bullet, possibly saving the life of the officer.

Search and rescue dogs

These dogs find people by scent. Some are brought into disaster areas to find people under rubble or in a dangerous situation, or they can be used to find people who are lost in the wilderness or disoriented. Some are trained to locate the scent in the air, while others are trained to track the scent on the ground. These dogs have been used following plane crashes or natural disasters. A team was also taken to the World Trade Center on 9/11, saving many lives.

Chapter 11

- Digging
- Barking
- Barking at door
- Biting objects
- Biting people
- Resource guarding
- Jumping

Fixing Bad Behaviors

When Fido is doing something that you don't want him to do, you must try to teach him what you want him to do instead. Rather than yelling at Fido when he is chewing on the couch leg, just say "Ahhh" and give him a Kong° or bone to chew on.

When Fido begins a bad habit, examine the situation and find the cause of the issue. Ask the following questions:

- Has Fido been exercised?

- Has Fido been mentally stimulated?

- Has Fido had plenty of human interaction throughout the day?

- Has Fido been reinforced for good behaviors often?

145

Digging

Fido may be digging to find prey, to escape, for entertainment or for protection. Determine what is the cause of Fido's digging, then try the suggested solution:

Prey: Small, underground animals will attract the attention of many dogs, especially terriers or hounds since that is the purpose of those breeds.

Solution: Try to rid your yard of the animals and take your dog on at least two walks per day. If Fido is a species bred to hunt prey, ridding your yard of the prey might be the only solution, as Fido is hard-wired to capture the animals.

Entertainment: If Fido gets bored and is left in the yard, he might decide to dig purely for enjoyment.

Solution: Be sure he has at least two walks each day or the equivalent of another type of exercise. Keep interesting toys in the yard for him, such as a filled Kong® and a bone or two. Have at least two training sessions each day to stimulate his brain.

Escape: If there is another dog or something interesting on the other side of a fence, Fido might be trying to get to it.

Solution: Extend the fence 2 feet underground, lay rocks along the fence line, bury chicken wire along the base of the fence or lay chicken wire or chain link beside the fence to discourage Fido from walking there.

Protection: Dogs sometimes dig in the dirt for protection from the weather, when they are too hot, or to be protected from harsh winds.

Solution: Bring Fido inside more often, and be sure he has adequate shelter and shade in the yard.

Barking

Puppies will experiment with barking, and it's best to stop it while they are young, before it's a habit. If Fido is young and barks for one of the first times, say "Ahhh" to interrupt him, then give him an incompatible behavior to do, such as "sit" "down" or "kennel."

If Fido has a habit of barking, then take Fido on at least two tiring walks each day to ensure he is getting adequate exercise. Then, try the following methods to stop the barking:

- *Ignore the barking.* Often, dogs will bark because it will get our attention. By ignoring the dog, we discourage the barking.

- *Remove the stimulus.* For example, if Fido is barking when people walk by the door, close or cover the door. If Fido is barking because he is playing, calm him down by putting him in his crate or putting him in a down-stay. Remove whatever is causing the behavior.

- *Ask Fido for an incompatible behavior.* For example, if Fido is barking because someone came to the door, then ask him to Place. He most likely won't be able to walk to his place and bark at the same time.

148

When Fido stops barking for a little while — between five seconds and one minute, depending on Fido's habit — reward him with a treat to encourage the silence. (Phase this out quickly, however, so he doesn't learn to bark, then stop just to get the reward.)

Barking at door

If Fido has a habit of barking when guests ring the doorbell or knock on the door, teach him to run to his kennel when he hears the doorbell, and in return he will receive a high-value reward. This is a great solution, as Fido is then out of the way and controlled for the guests that come in, and he is happy to do it. Below is an example of how to teach this:

Reward value: Best

Difficulty: Medium

Need to know: Crate training

❶ Ask someone to ring the doorbell or knock on the door (whichever Fido barks at).

❷ As soon as the sound is heard, give the command for "Kennel" in an extremely excited voice, then encourage Fido to run with you toward the kennel.

❸ When you both reach the kennel and Fido goes in, immediately reward.

❹ Give Fido's release word.

❺ Repeat Steps 1-4. *About 20 repetitions.*

149

Note: *During Step 5, if Fido comes out of the kennel without hearing the release word, close the crate door, just like you did during Crate Training. Throughout the steps, give Fido's release word after different amounts of time so he doesn't begin to anticipate it and will always stay in the crate until actually released.*

6 Gradually go less of the distance to the kennel with Fido, so he is eventually going to his crate by himself. Always M/R in the crate with a high-value treat and lots of praise. *Repeat each change in distance, about 5 repetitions.*

7 When Fido runs to the kennel on his own upon hearing the doorbell and your cue, gradually stop saying the cue, so he relies only on the sound of the doorbell.

8 Repeat Steps 1-7 from all rooms in the house. After learning the third or fourth room, Fido will probably generalize it to all rooms and won't need to go through all seven steps to know what to do.

When guests arrive for the first few times, excuse yourself and go reward Fido with four to five high-value treats if he has stayed in his kennel, then release him before he makes a mistake.

Even when Fido is proficient at this, always reward Fido with a high-value treat when he goes to his kennel in response to the doorbell.

Biting objects

Teething: Puppies go through stages, just like children, when they actually need to chew and bite on objects to soothe their gums.

Boredom: Fido might be chewing on furniture, rugs or shoes because he is bored and has nothing better to do. If he hasn't gotten enough exercise, the probability that Fido will chew out of boredom increases.

Solution: Make sure Fido has plenty of appropriate chew toys for chewing, of many textures and types. When Fido chews on something inappropriate, interrupt the behavior by saying, "Ahhh," then give him one of his chew toys instead. If he continues to chew on the unacceptable object, move him to a new area without the temptation and give him a chew toy.

151

Biting people (As mentioned in Chapter 3)

Biting is something everyone expects from a puppy, but it still hurts. Because of this, it's important to stop it ASAP so you and your pup can have a good relationship.

THERE ARE A FEW REASONS WHY PUPS WILL BITE PEOPLE:

Play

When puppies play with each other, they bite each other's ears, skin, etc., tackling and jumping on each other. Puppies must learn the appropriate way to play with humans. When Fido first comes home to you, he will not understand that he cannot bite you.

Teething

When puppies go through the teething stage, they are more prone to chewing on your fingers because it feels good to them.

If Fido is biting because he is playing or teething

Option 1: Say, "Ouch!" loudly in a high-pitched voice when his teeth touch your skin — even if it doesn't hurt, and freeze for five seconds. Then you may continue playing with Fido. After you have had to yell "Ouch!" three times, put Fido away — in his crate or on a leash without interaction from you. Then in 5 minutes or so, try to play with him again.

Option 2: When Fido's teeth touch your skin, say "Ouch" (Option 1), but also add a negative association with biting you. Since Fido is biting your fingers already, just hold his lower jaw — one finger on the inside of his mouth pressing down and one on the outside underneath, pressing up. Hold it firmly for approximately 3 seconds.

Fido will be uncomfortable and might try to squirm away, but keep holding until 3 seconds are up. Repeat this each time he bites your fingers.

If after a few repetitions, it hasn't discouraged him any, hold more firmly so it is a little more uncomfortable.

As with everything, teach Fido not to bite by starting very softly, and only increasing the intensity of the correction gradually and as needed.

Option 2 is cause and effect — pup bites, then pup feels discomfort. If this is done from the very beginning, the pup will know within a few days not to bite.

It is especially important to stop biting immediately in a family with children, as

puppies find that children are the most fun to gnaw on because the children squeal and want to play a game of chase when bitten — how fun! This makes for a very bad relationship between the child and dog.

153

Resource Guarding

Resource guarding may occur when you try to take away a valued object, such as a bone or his food, this needs to be stopped immediately! You must teach Fido that when you approach him, it is a good thing and not a threat. Do this by trading his object for something better. Then return his original object.

SPECIFIC INSTRUCTIONS:

1. Give Fido something he values, such as a bone, and let him chew on it for about a minute.

2. Walk up to him and put your hand out with your palm up.

3. With your other hand, give Fido a very high-value treat.

4. When he drops the bone to take the treat, pick up the bone.

5. When Fido swallows the high-value treat, give him back the bone.

Jumping

Begin teaching Fido not to jump the minute you bring him home (literally) by only petting him if he is sitting and ignoring him if he is not. It only takes about three days if done consistently. When trained properly, the pup simply runs up and sits in front of you, wanting attention. That is so much cuter than a dog that acts like a pogo stick every time someone walks in the door!

SPECIFIC INSTRUCTIONS:

❶ When Fido jumps on your legs, bring your hands up to your chest, stay still and look away from Fido. After a while, Fido will get off and do something else or sit and look at you in confusion.

❷ If Fido sits, give a reward and pet/praise him! If Fido doesn't sit, act as if nothing happened.

❸ Repeat Steps 1-2 each time Fido jumps up.

IF FIDO IS ALREADY IN THE HABIT OF JUMPING, TRY THE FOLLOWING STEPS:

❶ When Fido jumps on you, bring your knee up to his chest to cause him to get back on the floor.

❷ If Fido then sits, squat down and praise him. If he doesn't sit, ask him to sit. When he does, praise him.

❸ Repeat Steps 1-2 each time Fido jumps up. If after a few days Fido has not made any improvement, increase the intensity of your kneeing.

Chapter 12

- Hot dog chips
- Dried cheese
- Frozen p'butter treats
- Liver treats

Cookies

Some treats taste good and some taste *really* good — dog treats have different reward values. Their appeal often varies between dogs. I have one friend whose Basset will work just fine for a Cheerio, while some dogs like carrots or tomatoes.

For most dogs though, a good meat-based treat is the best; the closer to the pure meat the better. Dogs also seem to value "stinky" treats or very strong smelling meats and cheeses. However, this trait can be less than appealing when the scent lingers on your hands or in your treat pouch.

Speaking of treat pouches, it is a good idea to purchase one. Rewards need to be given immediately after the accepted behavior is completed. Having a treat pouch at your waistline ensures easy access. An alternative treat holder is a loose pocket, one that's easy to get in. This is sometimes hard to find with the new skinny jean phase of fashion. (Be aware, also, that treats can leave an oily stain on clothing.) The objective of the large pocket or treat pouch is to have the treat immediately available. What you don't want is to have to run into the kitchen and open the refrigerator to get a treat. In the time you have taken to do that your little pup will have forgotten what he did that he is being rewarded for.

Dried Meat

The treat I use most is left over meat. Whatever might have been the ends of dinner the night before I chop into pea size pieces and microwave for a few minutes, turning midway, until they are a dry "jerky" which will keep. Avoid the fatty sections and stay away from any salty portions, like the outside of a roast.

Frozen Dog Food

"Raw diet" dog food is also a great — and healthy — treat. Some brands sell bags of a little kibble size food nugget. They thaw quickly, so these are something to use at home right away and not to take along and put in your pocket.

Hot Dog Chips

Cut hot dogs into tiny pieces and spread out on top of a plate over a layer of paper towels. Microwave for 3 minutes. Turn over hot dog "chips" and microwave 2 more minutes. Cool and check to see if they are crunchy dry.

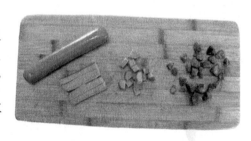

Dried Cheese

Cut block cheese into little pieces and leave out on cutting board for a day or two until it dries out and is crunchy. This works best in a low humidity environment.

Frozen P'butter Treats

1/3 cup peanut butter, microwaved for 30 seconds
2/3 cup plain yogurt

MIX yogurt and peanut butter until well combined. Drop small portions onto cookie sheet or wax paper and freeze until solid.

Liver Treats

1-20 oz. tub of chicken liver
3 eggs
2 ½-3 cups whole wheat flour
¾ cup plain yogurt

COOK the liver thru on the stovetop. Put the liver and remaining ingredients in a food processor, adding two cups of the flour last. Continue to add the flour while pulsing the mix, until it forms a dough ball.

GREASE a cookie sheet well. Pat and then roll out the dough onto a floured surface, adding flour as needed to prevent sticking. Use a pizza cutter or knife to cut the dough into small squares. Scoop onto the cookie sheet and bake at 400 for about 20 minutes or until firm and a bit crunchy. Turn over the treats and bake for another 10 min., or longer until these are crunchy and dried out like a cracker.

12

- Training schedule
- Shopping list
- Shot schedule
- Socialization list

Appendix

Example of a two-week training schedule for your new best friend

Day 1	Bonding	Crate Training	Name Game							
Day 2		Crate Training	Name Game	Come						
Day 3		Crate Training	Name Game	Come	Sit					
Day 4		Crate Training	Name Game	Come	Sit	Down				
Day 5		Crate Training	Name Game	Come	Sit	Down	Heel			
Day 6		Crate Training	Name Game	Come	Sit	Down	Heel	Sit-Stay		
Day 7				Come	Sit	Down	Heel	Sit-Stay	Watch Me	Stand
Day 8				Come	Sit	Down	Heel	Sit-Stay	Watch Me	Stand
Day 9							Heel	Sit-Stay	Watch Me	Stand
Day 10							Heel	Sit-Stay	Watch Me	Down-Stay
Day 11							Heel	Sit-Stay	Watch Me	Down-Stay
Day 12							Heel	Sit-Stay		Down-Stay
Day 13							Heel	Sit-Stay		Down-Stay
Day 14							Heel	Sit-Stay		Down-Stay

Shopping List

Collar

Buckle Collar: not a training tool, but perfectly suitable for your dog to have on for any training. This is what you put the I.D. tags on, or you can get one with the name and phone number on the collar itself – on a metal plate or embroidered into it.

Optional Training Collars

There are so many tools pet stores sell that "guarantee" your dog will walk perfectly by your side if used. I have yet to find one that actually makes your dog immediately learn to not pull on the leash — it's actually just up to you to teach your dog. There are tools that help, though. The following are descriptions of the primary tools available.

Harness with leash clip on the back
(Top Paw, Kong, etc.)

This teaches your dog to PULL YOU! Have you seen the harnesses on sled dogs or mules? The reason they have them on is to distribute the weight behind them, making it easier to pull the object. These dog harnesses are the same design and in your case, the object they are pulling is you, so these harnesses help Fido pull you to the next tree or fire hydrant he wants to sniff.

Head halter (Halti, Gentle Leader, Top Paw® HOLT)

Dogs hate these, because they are uncomfortable. If you want to use it, then you have to work to teach the dog to let you put it on, otherwise it will be a battle between you and your dog each time you have to take the dog outside. The head halter has the same effect as the harness with leash clip in front — if not actively being used to train the dog, then it is just a management tool, the dog isn't learning anything. If you actively train with it by rewarding the dog when he's walking calmly at your side, it can be a great tool. Once Fido knows how he should walk next to you, phase out the head halter so he can walk nicely with just a flat, buckle collar.

Harness with leash clip in front
(PetSafe Easy Walk, The SENSE-ation', The Wonder Walker™ Body Halter©)

While these may make the walk easier for you, they do not train Fido to stay beside you — they just redirect him so he can't pull. Because it is not training, it means for the next 15 years of your dog's life you will be required to have this harness on hand if you ever want to take your dog on a walk. If you are okay with not being able to take your dog on a walk without this tool, then that's fine, but I don't use it because of those limitations.

Prong/Pinch collar

These should only be used in extreme cases and when you have been educated on how to use them. The collar should only be on the dog under close supervision and during training sessions. The idea is that these collars are communicating cause and effect — Fido pulls and immediately gets a correction. Other options should be tried before this, but in the case of an extreme puller, pinch collars can be helpful, so that you are able to take the dog on a walk without getting leash-burned hands. It should only be used to correct the dog; a quick correction is given when the dog goes ahead of you, then there is immediate release. The dog shouldn't feel the collar unless a correction is being given. These can only be used on dogs over 1 year old, so the best option is to train your dog and just not let your dog get to this point.

Choke chain

This is a correction tool, rather than a preventive tool like the harness with leash clip in front or head halter. They are known to damage the dogs trachea, so I do not recommend them.

Slip collar

This is the same as the choke chain, but it is milder and are made of fabric, so they are less likely to damage the trachea. These are good for young dogs

that have moderate pulling because they cannot escape from the collar like with a buckle collar. When placed high on the neck and used only to correct the dog, the slip collar can be very useful.

Martingale

Basically, Martingales are combinations of slip collars and buckle collars. They give the same correction for pulling as a buckle collar (none), but they tighten up a little bit to keep Fido from escaping or just to let the dog know to pay attention to you. These are great collars for dogs that already know to pay how to heel, or for puppies that are just beginning to learn heel because the collar will tighten up to prevent them from accidentally escaping.

My preference is to use the slip collar or martingale, and train the pup to heel from a very young age. This way the collar is there for communication, i.e. to let the dog know to pay attention to you — if the pup needs it, but it is very mild. Also, it keeps the dogs safe by tightening up a little so they cannot back out of the collar like a buckle collar.

Leash

All that is needed is a 5-6 foot leash, fabric or leather. You may want to buy two or three so they can be by each door. That way if Fido needs to relieve himself then there is a leash readily available. No retractable leashes! Retractable leashes teach your dog to ignore slight tension on the leash – basically un-training them. They also are dangerous because you have no way to control Fido once he is far away from you. Additionally, because those leashes have wire/cord, they can get wrapped around a person and cause serious damage.

Food and Water Bowls

Any type of plain bowls will do. Ones with a larger base so they are unable to tip over are nice, but not mandatory. Don't use automatic feeders.

Dog Food

Ask your vet for what type of puppy food is best for your breed and size of puppy.

Toys

Have different textures of toys. Puppies explore the world through their mouths, and sometimes as they are growing and teething they want different textures. Some appealing textures are hard, rubber items such as a Kong, a stuffed animal, tennis balls or things that roll easily, or even bones of certain types like pig's ear, etc.

Crates

Soft Crate

Hard Crate

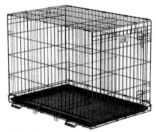

Wire Crate

Pet stores will try to sell you the "Taj Mahal" of crates, but it really comes down to a choice of soft, wire, or hard plastic crate.

For puppies, don't use a soft, fabric crate. Pups often get bored and chew their way out. These crates are fine for older dogs and convenient for travel because they fold down easily.

Both the wire and plastic crates are good for a puppy — indestructible! The plastic gives a more sheltered and cave-like effect for the puppy. This may make it feel safer. Because it is more sheltered there is no need to put a blanket over the top.

The wire is my personal favorite, though. The wire crates have a pullout tray unlike the plastic ones, which makes cleaning the kennel much easier if the dog is sick and happens to go potty in the crate.

Another benefit of the wire crates is that they often have dividers that can be put inside the kennel so that it can be made bigger as the pup grows. This is my favorite! When the pup is 8 weeks old, the crate needs to be much smaller than when he is 5 months old. The divider makes it so you do not have to buy 3 crates for your pup as he keeps growing. The downside of this crate is that there is no privacy, so if the crate is in an area of your house that is busy, a blanket will have to be put over it so that your pup can sleep without too many distractions.

Summary: Wire or plastic crates are good choices, but the advantage of wire crates is that they are adjustable, so you can make the crate bigger as your pup gets bigger.

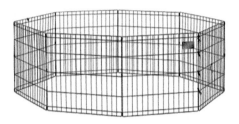

Exercise Pen (optional)

These are wire pens about 4 feet x 4 feet, that are sometimes helpful to contain the puppy without him having to be in his crate. I only use exercise pens outside on the grass, so that when pups go potty while in them, they are not being taught to go potty indoors. Don't use them inside the house unless the dog is house trained and won't make a mistake.

Baby Gates (optional):

These are sometimes helpful to contain Fido in certain areas of the house when he is a puppy. I have one blocking the laundry room entry, so this way I can put the pup in the laundry room for a few minutes to play, knowing exactly where he is. But, I only use this 30 minutes at a time, and only right after he has gone to the bathroom outside, so that I'm not teaching him that it is acceptable to relieve himself indoors.

Equipment Checklist

- ❑ 1 crate
- ❑ 1 buckle collar
- ❑ 1 training collar (optional)
- ❑ 2-3 leashes
- ❑ Food and water bowls
- ❑ Puppy food
- ❑ At least 4 different textures of toys
- ❑ 1 exercise pen (optional)
- ❑ Baby gates (optional)

Shot Schedule

Vaccinations can play an important role in keeping your puppy healthy, as puppies can be exposed to many deadly diseases. The first round of vaccines should begin when the puppy is between 6 to 8 weeks old, and the puppy should get three series of them, one every 3 to 4 weeks. Your puppy can get the rabies vaccine with the third set. On the following page is a suggested schedule.

6-8 Weeks: (DHPP) 4-Way with Distemper, Adenovirus (Hepatitus) Parvo, and Parainfluenza
- Intestinal Parasite Exam (Fecal)
- Begin a General Dewormer and repeat in 2 weeks

10-12 Weeks: DHPP
Possible vaccination with Leptospirosis and/or Bordatella, depending on your pup's lifestyle.

14 – 16 Weeks: DHPP
- Leptospirosis booster if needed
- Rabies vaccination
- Intestinal Parasite Exam
- Begin Heartworm Prevention

4-6 months: Spay or Neuter
- Microchip Implant

Yearly: Rabies vaccination
- DHPP

Thanks to Animal Hospital of Nicholasville, KY for a suggested schedule

Socialization Checklist

PEOPLE
- Different ethnicities
- Women
- Tall men
- Men with beards
- People wearing hats
- People wearing helmets
- People wearing big boots
- People with a hood on
- People wearing sunglasses
- People using a cane/ walker
- Teenagers
- Children petting them
- Children playing
- Toddlers
- People running
- Children in strollers
- Police officers
- Firemen
- People in costumes

OBJECTS
- Blow up objects
- Vacuum Cleaner
- Brooms
- Stairs
- Umbrellas
- Gym equipment
- Vending machines (loud noises)
- Alarms
- Doorbells
- Traffic
- Jack hammers
- Skateboards
- Bikes
- Cars
- Busses
- Motorcycles
- Rollerblades
- Shopping Carts
- Crutches
- Wheelchairs
- Balloons
- Garbage cans
- Garbage bags

ANIMALS
- Large dogs
- Small dogs
- Old dogs
- Puppies
- Cats
- Birds
- Cows
- Horses

SURFACES
- Concrete
- Brick
- Dirt
- Grass
- Gravel
- Sand
- Tile & other slippery floors
- Hardwood
- Carpet
- Metal (Vet scales)
- Grates (drainage, see through)
- Wobbly surface

169

Acknowledgments

I have many people to thank for helping me through the writing of this book. It was a huge project for me to undertake while still applying to college and attending high school. Without all their help it would never have happened.

Many thanks to Mr. Josh Fraley for going to bat for me, making it possible for me to write during school, even when it meant sacrificing his only planning period. This book would never have happened if I hadn't had that extra time. Thank you for overseeing my progress, and for having the confidence in me to allow me to be completely independent.

Mr. Bobby Beatty, I so appreciate you putting up with me — and my sarcasm — for far more than what was in your contract. And I thank you for the relentless teasing and mocking that you gave me each class, which always kept 4th period lighthearted and something I look forward to, no matter how behind on the book I was.

Thank you, Jeannie Francis Photography, for the stunning cover photo as well as the beautiful photo on the back cover. Thank you for your generosity and being so easy to work with. Your photos are amazing!

Acknowledgments

To Isaac, from Ibis Lagumbuy Art, the creator of Fido — I so appreciate your working with me as I asked for multiple random and confusing positions for Fido to be in. I'm extremely grateful that you put up with me continually adding more requests, while promising each was the last. To Joan Greenblatt of CenterPointe Media. Thank you for your encouragement, expertise, speed, patience, kindness, and great communication!

Without my first dog training instructor I would never have even trained a dog, much less been able to write this book. Sally Arias, I will forever be grateful to you for having enough faith in me, as a dinky eight-year-old, to handle your German Shepherd, Dillon. I cannot thank you enough for the high standards that you set for me and the opportunities I have had because of your teaching.

And lastly, I cannot express enough gratitude to my parents. Thank you for your constant support and encouragement. Thank you, Dad, for all the help hiring (and firing) and for finding just the right editors and formatters, and for your ever optimistic attitude — about the book and everything else. Mom, thank you for being my photographer, editor, ghostwriter, agent, etc. Thank you for being the artistic one and for trying to make the book more fun than I am! Thank you both, Mom and Dad, for allowing over 40 Comfort Retriever® puppies to go through our house in the past three years. Thank you for allowing me to follow my passion despite all the chewed furniture, puddles, noise, and mud that it entailed.

Author signing at the Lexington, Kentucky Farmers Market

Throughout the book, I showcase the Comfort Retriever®. The concept for this breed was conceived by Kathy Burgess. As a lifelong Golden Retriever fan, Kathy wanted to share the Golden's pleasant temperament and innate desire to please. Since many people find that Goldens are too big, shed too much, and have hip and health problems, she bred the world's first miniature Golden Retriever. The initial breeding with Cocker Spaniels did not rise to her demanding standards and produced puppies with temperament issues. Kathy eliminated the Cockers from the bloodline and added Poodle. She has been able to embrace Goldens' positive features and address the above issues and more through extensive genetic testing, strict breeding guidelines, and diversification. She continues to improve the Comfort Retrievers'® positive qualities through science. The Comfort Retriever® owners have become ambassadors for the breed, resulting in Kathy shipping the breed around the globe. You can find more information and images of the breed at www.ComfortRetrievers.com

Qualities of Comfort Retrievers®

- A comfortably sized family dog (20-55 pounds)
- Hypoallergenic
- Decreased shedding
- Increased longevity
- Both parents extensively health tested
- Wonderful temperament
- Intelligent and trainable
- Excellent with children and animals
- 100% lovable and family friendly

173

Index

Index

175

177

THE END

CPSIA information can be obtained
at www.ICGtesting.com
Printed in the USA
BVOW07s1137070716

454771BV00013B/32/P